LANGUAGE ARTS
MINI-LESSONS

*Step-by-Step Skill-Builders
for Your Classroom*

LANGUAGE ARTS MINI-LESSONS

Step-by-Step Skill-Builders
for Your Classroom

by Joan Clemmons and Lois Laase

SCHOLASTIC
PROFESSIONAL **B**OOKS

NEW YORK • TORONTO • LONDON • AUCKLAND • SYDNEY

TABLE OF CONTENTS

ACKNOWLEDGMENTS

I want to thank my students at Rolling Valley School for allowing me to include their pictures, comments, and work samples.

I'd also like to express thanks to Pat Liebentritt for her literature suggestions.

To my daughter, Stacie, for her encouragement and assistance in editing, I am grateful.

Most of all, I want to express my gratitude to my husband, Rod. Not only am I thankful for his love, support, encouragement, and patience, but I am very grateful for the generous assistance he gave me in writing. I benefited from his knowledge, suggestions, and his writing talent.

Joan

I wish to thank my students at Bookcliff Middle School and Wingate Elementary for allowing me to include their comments, work samples, and pictures.

I also want to express my appreciation to my whole family for their support and encouragement. A special thanks goes to my son Al for the many times he solved my problems with the computer.

And to my husband, Paul, I want to express my deepest appreciation for his enduring and enthusiastic support.

Lois

We both give special thanks to Carleen Payne and DonnaLynn Cooper who have shared so many wonderful teaching strategies with us, and who have always been there with their friendship and support.

To Liza Schafer and Terry Cooper, editors at Scholastic, we appreciate your belief in us as writers.

Lois and Joan

INTRODUCTION

This book is the product of a collaborative experience that began some eight years ago at Rolling Valley School in Fairfax County, Virginia. As teachers at Rolling Valley, we discovered a shared interest in and approach to using content to motivate children to acquire reading and writing skills. Although one of us taught second grade and the other taught fifth grade, and a flight of stairs separated our classrooms, we soon became a team, excitedly exploring ways that our similar teaching strategies could be adapted across grade levels. Together, we developed new approaches to effectively introduce and reinforce the skills that produce independent learners.

The opportunity to write this book came after we had moved thousands of miles apart, and we were delighted to find that distance had done nothing to diminish our friendship or our enthusiasm for refining the teaching strategies we had developed. In fact, we used our different settings to test the validity of our ideas. We adapted the lessons to fit students' needs and grade level curricula in second- through eighth-grade classrooms. The success that we had across grade levels, and with all types of children, made us more certain than ever that other teachers could benefit from using these approaches, too.

As we shared our ideas at teacher workshops, we became aware of the need for a book of mini-lessons on reading and writing strategies. Often during our presentations on portfolio assessment, teachers would ask how we taught the skills and strategies that produced the documents our students included in their portfolios. We usually only had time to respond with one or two examples, and it was difficult to walk away knowing that we hadn't given teachers all that they needed. This book has given us the chance to accomplish that, and we are grateful for the opportunity to organize and explain the many teaching strategies that we've developed during eight years of working together. We have taken care to offer the lessons that we think will be most helpful to other teachers.

Before we started writing, we made a list of the many different mini-lessons we enjoy teaching. From that list, each of us chose to write the lessons that show best how we use literature to teach a variety of skills and strategies in reading, writing, and grammar. Even though we divided the responsibility for primary authorship of each chapter, we continued working as a team. We communicated frequently as we each drafted the different lessons. We became experts in using electronic mail to communicate, sending whole lessons back and forth for one another to revise. The highlight of this writing experience was when we got together for separate, weeklong home visits and writing sessions. Our work was the most enjoyable when we brainstormed ideas to improve what we had written and then wrote for hours each day.

Our collaborative effort—over the telephone, up and down the information highway, and in intense work sessions—has been the most rewarding part of producing this book. Publication of these lessons gives us an even greater sense of collaboration because now our ideas will be used creatively by teachers all over this country.

We hope these mini-lessons will provide you with some new ways of using literature to teach language arts skills and strategies. Take our ideas and refine them to fit your classroom. Adapt them for use in teaching your students the curriculum at your grade level. And don't forget to share. Collaboration makes good teaching a universal experience.

Joan Clemmons   Lois Laase
Springfield, VA   Grand Junction, CO

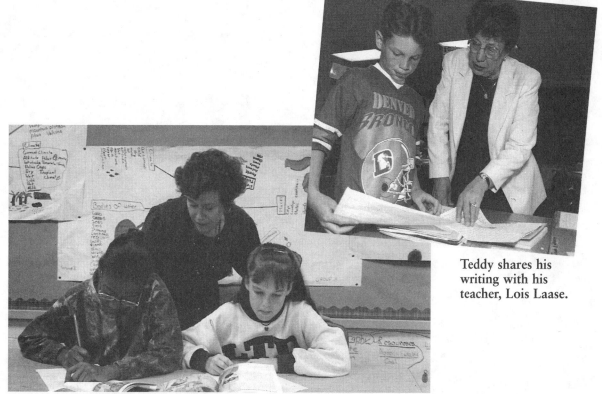

Teddy shares his writing with his teacher, Lois Laase.

Joan assists Elena and Carly with their research.

CHAPTER 1

How to Use This Book

Reading to learn and giving students a variety of writing experiences are central to our daily plans. In Chapter 2, "A Look at a Literature-Based Classroom," you will see a typical schedule that shows how we plan our day to include reading and writing activities in all subject areas. This chapter also provides a general picture of the elements of our literature-based classroom.

The subsequent chapters include 13 of our mini-lessons on using literature to teach skills and strategies in reading, writing, and grammar. Each lesson covers at least two, if not all three of the these areas, and each of our lessons can easily take several days to cover. So while we call them mini-lessons, they are certainly not miniature in their depth or in their effect on students' learning.

The literature selections that we use in each lesson either relate to a unit of study that our classes have pursued or are books we and our students have enjoyed reading. The lessons will have more meaning to your students if the literature you select is familiar to them. For example, we recommend that you use the book *Hatchet* as a resource for teaching skills only if your students are familiar with the story.

With so many new books published each year, not to mention the wonderful classics, it is not difficult to find literature to teach a specific skill. We continually browse through the children's section of bookstores and scour our libraries searching for literature that our students will enjoy and that we can use as a teaching tool. In the Question and Answer section of this book, Chapter 3, we give you a list of sources that will assist you in locating books pertaining to particular topics or genres.

As you read through our lessons you will notice that we always model what we expect from our students. When we model, we think aloud why and how we are doing certain things, with the expectation that students will learn from our examples. We simply do what we want them to be able to do, much as a ballet instructor might demonstrate a pirouette for her students. If, for examples, we want our students to learn how to write an effective paragraph, we write a paragraph on the blackboard and explain how we determine the main idea and the supporting details of the paragraph. We find that our students produce better work when we show them how we use the skills we want them to master.

Our lessons encourage student brainstorming, a situation in which students feel free to share their ideas. No student criticizes another for suggesting an unusual idea. We have the students work in small groups, and then the groups share their work. We use chart paper for recording the discoveries our students make, and leave the charts on display for students to refer to. The charts need not eat up all your precious wall space—they can be fastened to coat hangers and hung sideways on a chart rack, hung from the ceiling, or hung altogether on a hook.

As you read through this book, you will notice that the 13 mini-lessons are organized in the following manner:

1. the objective of the lesson,

2. an introduction,

3. a list of materials and preparations to complete before the lesson begins,

4. an explanation of the procedures for teaching the lesson,

5. follow-up activities for reinforcing the skill or strategy, and

6. various techniques for evaluating how individual students are using the skill.

We do not expect nor do we want you to follow these lessons step-by-step. To make them successful you will need to adapt them to your classroom needs.

CHAPTER 2

A Look at a Literature-Based Classroom

Make *reading-writing workshop a daily routine.* When our students have a set schedule and sufficient time to explore reading and writing, they take on more responsibility for their learning. For upper elementary and middle school students, we schedule an hour-and-a-half to a two-hour block of time for the workshop. We work closely with the administration and the special teachers, such as the music, physical education, and resource teachers, so that this block of time has as few interruptions as possible. On paper, the workshop is divided into a reading period and a writing period, but in reality, we use the time more flexibly. There are days when we devote two hours to reading and related activities, and days when we immerse ourselves soley in writing. The ample time block we've carved out enables us to develop lessons that flow logically from one activity to the next, and that are not confined by the dictates of a schedule.

We also integrate reading and writing across the curriculum. For example, if our students are writing reports for science, we may introduce lessons during writing workshop on note-taking and paragraph writing—skills that are at the heart of good science reporting. During science class, we weave reading into the hands-on experiment by modeling how to interpret scientific material. Throughout the year, we plan lessons that flow across the curriculum.

Let students know what is expected each day. We write our daily plan on the board each morning, so when students arrive they can see it. This helps keep them on task. A typical daily plan is shown below.

SCHEDULING THE DAY

Tuesday, November 8
Plans for the day

9:00–9:15
Morning activities

9:15–9:30
Read-aloud—Hatchet
◆ Will Brian get a fire started?

9:30–10:20
Reading workshop

Mini-lesson—author's point of view
◆ small-group activity

Independent reading
◆ Remember to record the name of your book.
◆ *My Side of the Mt.* novel group meets.

Reading response
◆ Discuss the point of view of the book you are reading.

Closure

10:20–10:30
Break

10:30–11:30
Writer's workshop
◆ Focus lesson—writing dialogue
    Discover rules for writing dialogue

Process writing
◆ status of the class
◆ drafting
◆ revising/peer conferences

Closure—Share your great writing

11:30–12:00
P.E.

12:00–12:35
Lunch and recess

12:35–1:35
Math—Continue with writing story problems.

1:35–2:15
Science—Take notes for research project.

2:15–2:25
Break

2:25–3:25
Social studies—group work on data retrieval chart

3:30
Dismissal

Again, schedules that are consistent help students know what is expected of them. We routinely plan for the following four activities just about every reading and writing workshop, in both upper elementary and middle school.

- ◆ We teach a mini-lesson that is applicable to the students' individual reading or writing.

- ◆ We give our students an opportunity to apply the lesson to their reading or writing.

- ◆ We allow students time to read for pleasure. Even if most of the workshop is devoted to writing, we give our students at least 20 minutes of sustained silent reading each day. Research indicates that students learn to read by reading; we must provide them with time in school to read.

- ◆ We always give closure to the lesson. For example, as a closing activity after a reading lesson—even an open-ended session of silent reading—we ask our students to write in their literature journals or talk about a book they are reading with other students. In writing workshop, the students often end the period by reading a few sentences or paragraphs from something they have written. Sometimes a student requests help from the peer group to solve a personal writing problem.

What Are Mini-Lessons?
When Are They Used?

Mini-lessons are focused sessions that teach the skills students need in order to become strategic readers and effective writers. The lessons are not prescribed, but arise out of our students' particular needs. We discover these needs as we work with them, and as we observe them at work. We watch, we take notes. During our reading and writing conferences we observe and record different student needs, and this helps us be aware of who needs additional assistance.

We usually teach these mini-lessons to small groups of students who display the same need based on these observations and our notes. For example, if we observe students needing help in reading comprehension, we would group them for lessons on comprehension strategies. Or, if we observe that a majority of students need help with a certain skill, such as how to write an effective lead sentence, then we present a focus lesson to the entire class.

In other focus lessons, we share information we feel our students need to tackle in a reading or writing task. For a unit on exploration,

we wanted students to organize their research with the help of a data retrieval chart. So after they had chosen an explorer to research, we taught a mini-lesson on how to write summary notes. Teaching the technique to students right when they needed it made the skill's value clear. Throughout the research process, we confer with students individually and in small groups, and teach and reteach the skills they need.

We teach reading and writing skills and strategies through the literature we read. We base our mini-lessons on the fiction and nonfiction that the students are reading, as well as on books we read aloud to them. In some mini-lessons, we also use the students' writings and/or our own writings as models. Using familiar, meaningful texts to teach skills and strategies engages students and helps them to understand that we are not teaching skills for skills' sake, but that skills matter, skills are relevant.

We teach in a way that reflects our district guidelines. As we use our school districts' curriculum guides in planning throughout the year, we integrate the reading and writing skills and strategies listed in the guides in all units of content studies. Teaching the skills when the students need them to achieve content goals is much more effective than teaching them in isolation or using worksheets as we may have done when we relied solely on basals. By teaching mini-lessons in varying contexts, we give students more opportunities to exercise the skills and eventually come to own them and to apply them independently.

We design mini-lessons to complement our students' interests, their self-evaluations, and the goals they set for themselves. Morgan, a 5th-grade student, wanted to write a letter to his congressman requesting a flag that had flown over the capitol. To aid him in drafting his letter, we presented a mini-lesson on how to write a business letter. Impromptu lessons like this give students the message that their learning goals matter to us.

Many of the lessons that we conduct during the first few weeks of the school year focus on classroom procedures. These lessons—which students have a hand in developing—provide students with routines that help them stay on task while we work with small groups or individuals. Students develop guidelines for routines such as giving book talks, writing in response journals, reading silently, borrowing books, and using the computer. These student-driven guidelines enrich the curriculum and provide a system of conduct that is essential to a successful reading and writing workshop.

Mini-lessons are based on:
- student need,
- student interest,
- student goals, and
- student objectives.

FLEXIBLE GROUPINGS

Heterogeneous grouping enhances students' self-esteem. When students with diverse abilities work together, everybody benefits. We frequently arrange our students into groups to work on an aspect of a particular lesson that everyone needs to practice. We form the groups quickly, so as not to waste valuable instructional time. We like to keep these heterogeneous groups together for at least four or five weeks so they have an opportunity to learn to work together. We then form new groups by changing the seating arrangement.

We seldom have students form their own groups. We want to include everyone. We sometimes have our students work in pairs. Stu-

dents sitting next to each other often work as partners, or we pair a confident reader with a less confident reader so one student can read to the other one. At other times we group two students together who have similar reading levels or interests. There are also times when we have the students choose their own partners; when we give students this option, we usually give them the option of working alone, too.

How we group, and the types of groups, depend on the task that needs to be accomplished. After observing that some of our students need help on a particular skill or strategy, we assemble them in groups. Research groups are based on interest—students interested in the animals of the rainforest, for example, will team up, while those who

want to focus on rainforest preservation work together. For literature, students form groups if they are reading the same novel or exploring the same genre.

Regardless of the purpose of the group and how the group is formed, the students must learn to work together. We, as teachers, always move from group to group modeling interaction skills. We might say, "Chris, that was an excellent idea," or "This group is right on target, they are all sharing ideas while Kim is writing them down as fast as she can." We also help the students stay on task and encourage everyone to be an active participant. At the end of the group activities, we ask students to spend a few minutes evaluating their accomplishments and interactive skills. Groups then set goals to improve their work next time.

READING EXPERIENCES

Daily Read-Alouds

Reading aloud to our students daily is an integral part of our curriculum. Students need to be exposed to many genres, so we read aloud at various times of the day, every day, even if it is just for a few minutes. At any grade level, reading aloud literature in the content areas enriches students' knowledge, expands their vocabulary, generates excitement about a topic, and incites lively discussions. For example, we often use the poem by Eve Merriam, left, to introduce a unit on the Civil War.

We also use read-alouds in our mini-lessons to enhance reading strategies and to model various writing techniques. For instance, we may choose to read aloud *The True Story of the Three Little Pigs* by Jon Scieszka (Penguin, 1989) to teach point of view; or *Hatchet* by Gary Paulsen (Puffin, 1987) to reinforce the skill of predicting; or *Mummies, Tombs, and Treasure* by Lila Perl (Clarion, 1993) to explore expository writing. We also use read alouds to study how setting influences plot, as well as how authors develop characters. For the mini-lessons, we often put key pages of an author's work on transparencies, and work as a class to determine what makes the writing work. The students then use it as a model for their own writing.

> **TO MEET MR. LINCOLN**
>
> *If I lived at the time*
> *That Mr. Lincoln did,*
> *And I met Mr. Lincoln*
>
> *With his stovepipe lid*
> *And his coalblack cape*
> *And his thundercloud beard,*
> *And worn and sad-eyed*
> *He appeared:*
>
> *"Don't worry, Mr. Lincoln,"*
> *I'd reach up and pat his hand,*
> *We've got a fine President*
> *For this land;*
>
> *And the Union will be saved,*
> *And the slaves will go free;*
> *And you will live forever*
> *In our nation's memory."*
>
> *Eve Merriam*

Choosing Books for Independent Reading

One of the first mini-lessons we present is how to select a book, as some students are not used to choosing literature. We let them know that it's fine to reread favorite books, or read them aloud to others. While these books may be easy for them, rereading enhances students' self-confidence, reinforces reading strategies, and reminds them of the pleasure of reading. Of course, we encourage students to read plenty of books that are new to them and more challenging. We also point out that there are books that they will find very difficult to read, and that it's okay to stop reading a book if it's too frustrating.

We also discuss our own reading habits, revealing that adults, too, read at a variety of levels. Sometimes we read something easy, such as a magazine. Other times we read novels that are entertaining and just right. We also read professional material which can be harder to read and comprehend. The students need to know that we as teachers make the same choices when selecting reading material.

We take time to introduce students to the new books in our classroom collections. We give brief talks about them and use the book jackets to help us introduce those we haven't read. Periodically, we arrange to take our students to the library and have the librarian give book talks about new books or introduce ones that pertain to our current unit of study. Students readily learn about books from each other, through book talks, literature groups, and more informal conversations. Often a favorite book is passed around the room and read by a number of students. This is perhaps the most powerful motivator of all.

We have students who start new books and after reading a few pages say, "I don't like this book. It isn't good." For these students we explain that authors may give background information in the first chapter and also possibly in the second chapter. The action may not start until the third chapter. We encourage them to remain with a book until they have read the third or maybe the fourth chapter. Students will often say, "You were right. This book is good now."

Record Keeping

We ask students to keep a record of the books they read (see example on page 21). In addition to reading in the classroom, students are expected to read for at least 30 minutes at home each day, and to record the date, title, author, genre, and the page numbers they begin and end on. This running record helps students—and us—evaluate their reading habits, anwering such questions as: What time of day do I read? Am I reading enough? What kind of books do I like best? What genres do I need to try?

Novel Groups

Novel groups are another good venue for reading literature and presenting mini-lessons. Together, groups of students explore a theme, a genre of literature, or an author. After we introduce the theme, genre, or author to our students, we share with them three or four novels related to the topic of study. We have multiple copies of the novels available, and students form groups based on which novels they wish

LIST OF BOOKS

Name _____

Date	Books I Have Read	Author	Pages	Type of Literature

to read. (The number of copies of each book also determines the size of the groups.) We guide these heterogeneous groups to discuss the novels in terms of theme, character, setting, plot, author's style of writing, and so on.

WRITING EXPERIENCES

We give our students time to write every day. We have them write for many purposes. They write in the content areas. They write about what they are learning in their learning logs. In their reading journals they write responses to the literature they read.

Our students write independently. One of our first mini-lessons in independent writing involves the students in brainstorming possible topics for writing. They make a list of their ideas and keep it in their writing folders to use for inspiration.

We often link literature and creative writing. For example, when reading folktales, our students write their own folktales or rewrite a classic one from the point of view of a particular character.

Our students learn the writing process. We familiarize students with the stages of the writing process through mini-lessons. In the prewriting stage, children brainstorm ideas and organize their thoughts. If they are trying to write about an unfamiliar topic, they may spend prewriting time researching and gathering information. Students **then** draft and revise. We encourage them to confer with their peers and with us as they rewrite. We have found that our students need to be shown through our modeling how to revise their writing.

Pendulums

Look, Look! see them dine
Dancing like they were alive
Over, under all around.
Never does it touch the ground
Swaying here, Swaying there
Swinging, swaying everywhere.

by: Emily

Emily used the writing process to create her poem.

CRITERIA CHARTS FOR WRITING

I hear and I forget.

I see and I remember.

I do and I understand.

As we develop lessons, we make a point to involve students so that they can *see* and *do,* which helps them to *remember* and *understand.* For example, after a lesson on writing an effective paragraph, we ask students to define the criteria and list them on a chart (see the lesson on writing paragraphs from summary notes, Chapter 6). The chart reminds them to use vivid words, to have a topic sentence, to stick to the topic, and so on. As we explore paragraphing further, we add new criteria to the chart. As a class, we develop other criteria charts as we study story writing, report writing, poetry, and so on. Collectively, the charts—displayed around the classroom—provide students with an at-a-glance manual of good writing. Later, students use the

23

charts to help them evaluate their own work and set goals for themselves as writers.

EVALUATION

Evaluation in our classrooms is an ongoing process. Earlier in our teaching careers, we assessed students' final products in order to assign grades on papers and in our grade books. Since then, our concept of student learning and understanding has evolved. Now we see that assessment and instruction are woven into one, and that it's not the final products that matter most, but the students' progress along the way. So we continually observe our students and evaluate the skills and strategies they are using in the reading and writing processes. As we measure and note their abilities, we provide whatever instruction is needed. We write anecdotal notes recording the skills and strategies students have command of and those that need strengthening. We use these notes to plan future mini-lessons. In other words, our teaching is based on a cycle of observation, planning, instruction, and evaluation.

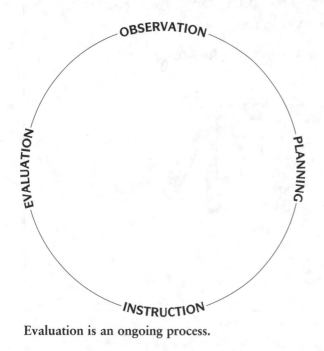

Evaluation is an ongoing process.

Our students participate in the evaluation process. They record the books they read and their personal responses to them, and use these notes to evaluate the type and quality of literature they are reading. In our mini-lessons, we encourage students to discover the criteria or standards for effective writing. Not only do the students use these criteria to aid them in writing, but they use them to help self-evaluate their work and set goals for improvement. Quarterly, they select samples of their work in reading and writing, self-evaluate them, and include them in their portfolios. Because our students collaborate with us in the evaluation process, they assume more responsibility for their learning and are motivated to achieve their goals.

CHAPTER 3

Questions and Answers

As we give our workshops across the country we frequently hear the same concerns and questions. We tried to address most of the concerns in this book, but the following specific questions are answered here.

1. How do you decide on the literature that you use for a particular lesson?

Since there are so many wonderful books available, it is hard to decide which ones to use. Before we teach any unit of study, such as Egypt or the American Revolution, we search for literature relating to that topic. If we want to teach a particular genre, we look for books of that genre. The first person we go to is the librarian in the public or school library. With the librarian's help, we search through the card catalogue or computer to determine available resources. Some reference books list books under different topics—two that we use frequently are *A to Zoo* and *Children's Books in Print*. Many professional books have wonderful booklists. We refer to these sources when we are looking for specific literature. Some of the books we use most frequently are the following: *Your Reading, A Booklist for Junior High and Middle School*, edited by C. Anne Webb (NCTE, Urbana, IL; 1993); *Using Nonfiction Trade Books in the Elementary Classroom* (Freeman & Person, NCTE, Urbana, IL; 1992); *Invitations* by Regie Routman (Heinemann, Portsmouth, NH; 1991); *Teens' Favorite Books* (International Reading Association, Newark, DE; 1992); and *Hey, Listen to This: Stories to Read Aloud* by Jim Trelease, (Penquin Books, New York; 1992). Whenever we find a book that we particularly like we make a note of its title and the pages that we want to use.

2. When I go into a library, I do not know where to look for books that are suitable for my grade level. How can I help my students locate good literature when I don't know what is available myself?

We know that feeling. We go to the library and look at the bookshelves and say: Where do we begin? What books will interest our students? Librarians are wonderful help. They provide us with updated Newberry Award booklists, direct us to the newest books on the shelves, and provide us with books related to our unit of study.

We also keep our ears and eyes open. By noticing the books some of our students are reading and by listening to their book talks, we expand our knowledge of book titles. We also use the professional books listed in the previous answer as sources.

3. Where do you get the creative ideas for your lessons?

We read and we brainstorm ideas. We are always on the lookout for new ways to teach the school district's objectives, units of study, and the topics our students show a need for or interest in. Some of the professional magazines that we find helpful are the following: *The Reading Teacher* and the *Journal of Reading* published by the International Reading Association; *Language Arts* and *English Journal* published by the National Council of Teachers of English; and *Arithmetic Teacher* and *Mathematics, Teaching in the Middle School* published by National Council of Teachers of Mathematics. Our best ideas come from sharing with each other and with other teachers, and from our students.

4. When you teach skills and strategies through mini-lessons, how do you know that you have covered all the objectives that your school district requires?

After we teach a thematic unit or study a specific genre, we go through our school district's objectives and check off those that were included in our study. We note those that we need to include in our plans the next time. Another approach is to plan a unit with specific objectives in mind. But addressing an objective does not mean that the students have mastered that skill and can use it as an effective strategy. Most skills and strategies need to be modeled and taught repeatedly, either to the whole class or in small groups.

5. I always thought anecdotal notes were a good way to record behavior. How do you use them for evaluating students' work?

When we read what our students have written and observe them at work, we record brief comments, noting the skills and strategies they use, as well as those for which they show a need. We write positive comments stressing their strengths on the students' papers. We give specific praise when we see a job well done. Putting a grade on a paper and recording it in a grade book does not serve a purpose unless you know why the student received that grade. In the anecdotal notes we can chart the student's progress as well as note his needs. We have to know the needs of our students to plan future instruction.

After experimenting with several methods for keeping anecdotal records, we found one that works the best for us. We divide a sheet of paper into sections and put a student's name in each section. Using this as our master copy, we reproduce it. We use a new sheet each time we evaluate what the students have written or observe our students in a meaningful learning experience. These notes make it easy to pull certain students together for small group focus lessons. (See example on page 28.)

6. What do the other students do when you work with a small group?

There are many reading and writing activities that students can do while you work with a small group. Our students read silently; respond in their journals to the literature they are reading; or work on art, music, or drama projects that relate to their reading. They pursue writing projects using the writing process. For instance, they do research on a specific topic, draft new pieces of writing, confer with peers, or publish a piece of writing.

The key to keeping students on task is the modeling and planning we do at the beginning of the year. We start with focus lessons that concentrate on procedures. Our students learn how to move from one activity to the next without help. They learn to function independently.

One year I had a group of students who had difficulty staying on task. When I finished meeting with small groups and before we began another activity as a whole class, I asked the students to write what they had accomplished on their own and to discuss their behavior. I had these students evaluate their behavior frequently. Also, posting a list of tasks helped some students move from one activity to another. These ideas became useful tools in classroom management.

ANECDOTAL RECORDS

Topic _Writing Conferences_ Date _January 15_

Adam	Amy	Betsy	Bob
Using possessives correctly. Needs help on run on sentences.	Working on draft on horse report — great research notes		Suggested he use thesaurus to help him with vocab
Brandi	**Cathryn**	**Cobb**	**David**
	Discussed how peer editors helped with revising — Great feedback.		Needs help with revising — Tomorrow's task
Elizabeth	**Fletcher**	**Gary**	**Howard**
	Making a web 2nd day — tomorrow he writes	Howard gave him lots of peer editing help — work on paragraph flow.	
Ike	**Jane**	**Kathy**	**Lance**
Publishing — using computer	Help needed on sentence structure — great ideas in story	Still having difficulty with caps — Story really flows	
Megan	**Paul**	**Sarah**	**Tom**
	Help needed on verb tenses		Having trouble coming up with story ideas

7. *What are the different ways students can respond to literature?*

To answer this question we would have to write another book! Having our students respond to the literature they have read is an important part of our program because the process aids the students in the acquisition of comprehension strategies. However, it is important to remember that students need to enjoy literature. If we do too many activities with a book, students may lose interest in it and thus in reading. Our goal is to develop lifelong avid readers who appreciate literature.

There are so many ways to respond to literature. I find that after I model some of the types of responses for my students, they are creative with their own ideas. Without going into any detail, here are ten different ways to respond to literature. They may act as a springboard to help you and your students develop other methods.

- ◆ Compare one book to another.
- ◆ Retell the story from a personal point of view.
- ◆ Act out the story.
- ◆ Use puppets to tell the story.
- ◆ Write a letter about the book to a friend.
- ◆ Write a letter to a character.
- ◆ Write a story patterned after your book.
- ◆ Draw a picture that shows the setting and characters.
- ◆ Compare the main character to someone you know.
- ◆ Write a play based on the story.

8. *How can I involve students who are reading below grade level?*

Most of these students probably understand when the books are read aloud, so more than likely it is not the comprehension that is difficult for them, rather the reading. These students can listen to books on tape, have an adult read to them, or even have another student read to them. It is also important that the teacher read aloud to the students every day. With a good literary background these students can meet with success instead of defeat. In fact, we know several students who have been spurred on to develop their reading skills after working with us on these focus lessons. Reading now has a purpose for them.

CHAPTER 4

Comprehension Strategies

OBJECTIVE   Students will enhance their reading ability by thinking comprehension skills out loud.

There is a popular notion that children who become better readers also become better thinkers. I have found the converse to be true, as well; children who become effective thinkers also become effective readers. This was the case with Kristen, whose reading ability vastly improved by the end of the school year. Best of all, she developed an enthusiasm for reading, as she attests in this reflection on her reading in her portfolio:

> In September I was a very slow reader and couldn't understand most of the books I read. I used to read only half an hour a day. Now I can read a little faster, and I can understand what I am reading. I usually read at least two hours a day, one hour after school and another hour before I go to bed. I really love to read. I am using the reading strategies now because we practiced thinking them out loud many times this year.

The most powerful tool for improving reading comprehension is *metacognition*, the awareness of the thought processes one is using. When we foster this awareness in a child, we are cultivating a strong reader and thinker. The following example will illustrate what I mean.

Decision-making is a thinking skill children use many times a day. They decide what to wear, what to eat, with whom to talk, whether to share a toy, and so on. Frequently, we give them clues about how they are faring with this skill by telling them that they made bad or good decisions. But this approach is a very clumsy way to teach decision-making because the student has to guess what is on the teacher's mind, and the teacher has to spend a great deal of time qualifying decisions.

With so many things to accomplish in the classroom, the time for inferential learning is limited; teaching metacognition provides a great shortcut. Here are the parts of the decision-making skill I outline for students:

- recognizing an occasion for a decision,

- gathering information,

- considering alternatives and possible outcomes,

- selecting the alternative that best suits one's goal, and

- evaluating the result.

What's metacognition? Thinking about thinking by the thinker.

Each time there is an opportunity to label a decision good or bad, I instead have the student consider the steps in the process, identify which steps were left out or misapplied, and state how a better decision could have been made. With practice, students learn to stop and think about their decision-making *before* the decision is made.

DECISIONS READERS MAKE

Not every student becomes an able decision-maker right away. But the more serious decisions are made more deliberatively and with better results. This improvement occurs because I have taken the mystery out of what I mean by good and bad decisions and have applied energy to *teaching* instead of *labeling*. You can apply this same technique to teaching reading comprehension. Here is how I make the thinking skills of good readers a part of every child's metacognition.

MODELING METACOGNITION

I model metacognition by thinking out loud. I verbalize what I am doing—questions I have, my hypotheses, the steps I am using to solve a problem, or the thoughts I have about the topic. Children literally hear me work through difficulties I may have with the text. This is a technique I used for years in teaching math, but I never thought about employing it in the teaching of reading until Carleen Payne, a reading specialist, demonstrated it in my class one day. This strategy also appears in professional literature as a highly recommended way to improve comprehension skills (Beth Davey, *Journal of Reading*, October 1983; James Flood and Diane Lapp, *The California Reader*, Fall, 1992). As I continue to use think-alouds with students, I find ways to refine the technique. Here is a blueprint of how I go about presenting the lesson. You will naturally adapt it to fit the needs of your students.

How I Do It

My students are familiar with most of the reading strategies at the time I give this lesson. They have had previous experience with prediction, thinking about what they already know about a topic, visualizing, and using context clues. They have also had practice retelling stories orally and in writing.

Before asking students to think out loud as they read, I model the procedure for them. I prepare by flagging passages in the book I am reading out loud that call upon various reading strategies. The flags (sticky notes work well) remind me to stop and think out loud the strategy I am using. I also make a checklist of the strategies I want students to use (see Strategies That Good Readers Use, page 34), distribute a photocopy to each student, and make a transparency of it to use on the overhead projector during the demonstration.

I also select the texts I want students to read as they think out loud various reading strategies. The material is always at their instructional reading level. If I plan to emphasize only two or three of the strategies at a time, I select a story that elicits those strategies. I often use stories in the basal readers as well as other short stories and trade books. If we are studying a particular genre, I will use books within the genre for this activity.

SETTING THE STAGE

I introduce the technique to students by explaining that as I read aloud, I will be thinking out loud as I read. To help students relate the technique to something they already do, we discuss how sometimes we talk to ourselves as we work through a problem. I point out that

STRATEGIES THAT GOOD READERS USE

Reader's Name _____

Title of Text_____

Listener's Name_____

LISTENER'S CHECKLIST

Did the reader verbalize these strategies? Place a check next to the strategy each time it is used.

Before Reading

◆ Think about what he/she already knows about the topic.   _____

◆ Predict what the text will be about or what will happen next.   _____

While Reading

◆ Ask questions.   _____

◆ Look for answers to questions.   _____

◆ Guess or predict what will happen.   _____

◆ Check guesses or predictions.   _____

◆ Relate what is being read to prior knowledge.   _____

◆ Check for meaning by rereading the parts that aren't making sense.   _____

◆ Use context clues to determine a new word or meaning of a word.   _____

◆ Retell parts of the text.   _____

◆ Describe the pictures made in his/her mind.   _____

After Reading

◆ Summarize or retell the important things in the text.   _____

Listener's Comments: _____

_____

_____

we often do this when we are working on something that has many steps, such as a science experiment or a recipe. Thinking out loud helps us when we want to make sure we don't omit anything.

I ask if anyone can recall doing something that prompted him or her to say the steps aloud. A student might share how he prepares for school by reciting all the items he is packing in his backpack, or how he talks aloud when he is assembling a model, or working on the computer.

I point out that we often verbalize our thinking as we solve math problems. To illustrate this, we talk through the steps of solving a division problem: "I want to divide 436 by 9. I think: Are there any 9s in 4? No. Are there any 9s in 43? Yes, 5. No, 5 times 9 is 45. So there are 4. 4 times 9 is 36. 43 minus 36 is 7. Bring down the 6. How many 9s are in 76? There are 8 because 8 times 9 is 72. 72 from 76 is 4. 4 is the remainder." We said aloud or thought aloud the steps as we divided.

I explain to students that we can also think out loud as we read, to help us learn strategies that we can use when we read silently. These strategies will help us understand and remember more of the material we read.

TALKING OUT THE TEXT

I place on the overhead projector the Strategies That Good Readers Use transparency (see page 34). I explain that good readers use these techniques to make sense of the text. I discuss each strategy with them. To help you explain the reading strategies to your students, you might try defining each one as follows.

STRATEGY: Think about what he/she already knows about the topic.

EXPLANATION: Before we read, we should look at the title, author, and pictures and think about what we already know about that topic or story.

STRATEGY: Predict what the text will be about or what will happen next.

EXPLANATION: Based on the title, pictures, and the information we already know about the topic, we need to make predictions about the story or the topic before we start reading.

STRATEGY: Ask questions and look for answers.

EXPLANATION: While we are reading, we need to stop and ask ourselves questions about the text we are reading and look for answers to the questions.

▲ ▲ ▲ ▲ ▲ ▲

Explain and model the reading strategies to your students, so they can understand how to use them effectively as they read.

▼ ▼ ▼ ▼ ▼ ▼

STRATEGY: Guess or predict what will happen.

EXPLANATION: Based on what we have read or already know, we guess or predict what will happen next.

STRATEGY: Check guesses or predictions.

EXPLANATION: As we read, we check our guesses or predictions. We revise them or make new ones.

STRATEGY: Relate what is being read to prior knowledge.

EXPLANATION: We relate what we are reading to our prior knowledge. That is, we think about how something that is happening in the text is like something we already know.

STRATEGY: Check for meaning by rereading the parts that aren't making sense.

EXPLANATION: If the text is not making sense, we stop and reread those parts. We think about the words and what they mean.

STRATEGY: Use context clues to determine a new word or meaning of a word.

EXPLANATION: When we come to a new word, we can use context clues to figure out its meaning. We use the words around it or read on and use the sense of the text to figure out its meaning.

▲ ▲ ▲ ▲ ▲ ▲

Depending on the level of your students, you may want to have them focus on just two or three of the strategies at a time until you have worked through all of them.

▼ ▼ ▼ ▼ ▼ ▼

STRATEGY: Retell parts of the text.

EXPLANATION: We stop periodically to check our understanding of what we've read by retelling the part of the text that we've read. If we can't retell it, we reread it and then retell it to ourselves.

STRATEGY: Describe the pictures made in his/her mind.

EXPLANATION: As good readers, we make pictures in our mind of what we are reading. We visualize the descriptions, the characters, the settings, and the events in the plot.

STRATEGY: Summarize or retell the important things in the text.

EXPLANATION: When we stop reading, we summarize or retell the important things in the text that we have read.

MODELING THE STRATEGIES

Now I explain that I will stop reading periodically and verbalize what I am thinking. I want students to participate by listening and identifying the strategy I am using. They are then to come to the overhead projector and check it off on the checklist. As I read aloud from *Pigs Might Fly* by Dick King-Smith (Scholastic, 1980), the dialogue in my classroom sounds something like this:

MRS. C: I have chosen to read *Pigs Might Fly* by Dick King-Smith. I know that pigs can't really fly, so this must be a fantasy since that is the type of literature that has animals or objects talking and doing things that can't really happen. I also know that pigs are supposed to be rather intelligent animals. From the picture on the cover I see that a pig appears to be flying over a farm. Maybe the pig is the main character and imagines he can fly. I predict that he will use that fantasy to help him solve the problem in the story.

(Usually by this time many students have raised their hands to participate. If they haven't, I invite them to tell me which strategies they hear me using.)

CARLY: You thought about what you already knew about pigs and stories. You also looked at the picture and predicted what the story will be about.

(Carly then comes to the overhead projector and places check marks next to the first two strategies listed.)

MRS. C: Chapter One is entitled "Taken Away." Who is taken away? I can see in the picture a tiny pig in a pen with a large hog. Is one of them going to be taken away?

BRIAN: You asked questions.

(He then places a check mark next to that strategy on the transparency, and I continue to read aloud.)

MRS. C: *"Oh, no!" cried Mrs. Barleylove miserably. "Oh no!" "What is it, dear?" came the voice of Mrs. Gobblespud next door. "One dead?" "No," said Mrs. Barleylove. "Not yet anyway."* The little pig must be sick. He must be the one that is going to be taken away.

ELENA: You guessed and predicted what will happen next.

(She places a check mark next to that strategy.)

MRS. C: *Mrs. Barleylove was a pedigree Gloucester Old Spots, a* *flop-eared white pig spotted with black blobs of color, as though a giant had flicked his paintbrush at her.* I can picture this very large black-and-white sow with a curly tail, grunting as she walks around the barnyard.

JULIE: You described the picture in your mind.

(She checks off that strategy on the transparency.)

MRS. C: *During the night she had given birth to eight babies, seven of them all of a size, round and strong-looking and already plumped out with their first milk. But the eighth, she now saw, was a poor spindly...* What does *spindly* mean? The sentence began with the word *but*, which means an opposite idea. So it would be opposite of *round* and *strong-looking*, which are the words the author used to describe the other babies. I think I'll read on. *...spindly little creature, half as big as the rest, with a head too large for its scrawny body and a look of hopelessness on its face.* From the sentences, I can tell that *spindly* means very little or thin, scrawny or frail.

ALLISON: You used context clues to figure out the meaning of spindly.

(She marks the strategy on the transparency.)

MRS. C: *It was a runt, a piglet born for some reason far smaller and weaker than its brothers and sisters.* That reminds me of my cat. She was the runt, or the smallest kitten in her litter.

BIANCA: You related what you were reading to prior knowledge.

(She checks off the strategy.)

MRS. C: *In different parts of England they are called by different names—cads, wasters, or nesslegraffs. In Gloustershire they call them dags.* So dags are runts, and the setting of this story is a farm in England.

AMY: You used context clues to tell the meaning of *dags* and where the story is taking place.

(She places a check mark next to that strategy.)

MRS. C: *There was a rustling and a scrabbling in the next sty, and Mrs. Gobblespud's head appeared over the wall. "Oh, dear me," she said. "Oh, dear me, Mrs. B. Oh, I am sorry. It isn't just a small-ish one, is it?" "No," said Mrs. Barleylove. "It's a real dag."* The pigs seem to be very worried that one of the baby pigs is a dag, or runt. Are they worried that he is so little and frail? Or will he be the one taken away?

JANE: You asked questions.

(She checks off that strategy on the transparency.)

MRS. C: *Most of the Old Spots sows in the range of nine sties had probably had a dag at some time in their careers as mothers. It wasn't thought of as a disgrace, something to be whispered about, because it didn't seem to be anyone's fault. But it was thought to be a pity, a great pity, for every sow's ambition was to rear a fine litter of healthy, evenly matched youngsters, and as the news spread that morning, there was much worried grunting and rolling of eyes and shaking of long, droopy ears.* I was correct. The sows are worried that a dag, or runt, was born because they want all of the litter to be healthy ones.

PETER: You checked for answers to your questions.

(He places a check mark next to that strategy on the transparency.)

MRS. C: *The servant wouldn't like it either, they said to each other. They thought of the Pigman as a servant since he did nothing but minister to their wants; he fed them, he watered them, he cleaned them out and brought fresh bedding. They spoke of him—and to him, though he could not understand this—simply as "Pigman," as a Roman nobleman might have said "Slave."* This part doesn't make sense. I need to reread it and think about what I am reading. (I reread the text stated above.) Now I understand it. The pigs refer to the person who takes care of them as Pigman. Since he does everything for them in taking care of their needs, they think of him as their servant or slave.

KISHA: You reread the part that didn't make sense to you, and you retold that part.

(She places check marks next to those strategies on the checklist.)

MRS. C: *Pigman wouldn't be pleased about Mrs. Barleylove's dag, for dags, if they survived, grew very, very slowly and were more trouble than they were worth. Pigs Might Fly* is a fantasy that is taking place on a farm in England. During the night a litter of baby pigs was born to the sow, Mrs. Barleylove. One of the eight pigs was a spindly runt that they call a dag. All of the sows are very worried that a dag was born because they like for all of their pigs to be healthy ones. The pigs refer to their caretaker as Pigman. He will not be happy that a dag was born because he thinks they are more trouble than they are worth. I predict that Pigman will take the dag away. However, the dag might "fly" away from the Pigman.

CHRIS: You summarized or retold the important things that you read and predicted what will happen next.

(He places check marks next to those strategies on the transparency.)

MRS. C: The bottom of the checklist has space for the listener to write comments. What can you say about how I used the reading strategies?

Carly places a check mark next to the strategy.

ALAN: You used the strategies on the checklist. That gives me ideas for using them when I read.

LISA: You understood what you read.

STUDENTS TAKE A TURN

When I've finished modeling, I explain to the students that I want them to use these strategies automatically when they read silently to help them understand the text. I tell them they're going to have a chance to talk out their reading strategies just as I did.

I give students a copy of the Strategies That Good Readers Use checklist, and then arrange students in pairs according to their instructional reading levels. (I group them as such because I want them to read the same material.) I tell students that they are going to take turns reading aloud for about ten minutes, while their partners listen. The readers are to stop reading periodically and think out loud just as I did. The listener's job is to check off the strategies the reader uses on his checklist. If the reader uses a strategy more than once, she should check it each time it is used. If the reader does not use any of the strategies, the listener may suggest strategies for the reader to try. At the end of the period the listener should write positive comments about how the reader used the strategies.

As the pairs practice verbalizing the reading strategies, I rotate from group to group—listening and giving praise, encouragement, and guidance. I also serve as the timekeeper, telling students when they have about three minutes left of reading aloud, and reminding them when it is time to switch roles.

STACIE THINKS OUT LOUD

I sat with Stacie and Andrea as Stacie verbalized her thoughts while reading *The Whipping Boy* by Sid Fleishman (Greenwillow, 1986).

STACIE: (reading the text) *The last mischievous deed that Prince Brat decided to do was to run away from the castle. He said he was bored, and he forced whipping boy, Jemmy, to go with him and carry his basket. They became lost as they were riding the horse through the fog and were captured by two villains who wanted to rob them. The villains took the horse and basket and told the boys to go away. Before they got away, one of the villains discovered the king's crest on the saddle.*

I predict that the villains will now believe that the prince is who he really says he is and will not allow them to leave. They will probably demand money for their release.

(Stacie continues reading.)

"We stole it, horse and saddle!" Jemmy put in desperately.

"Bosh!" retorted Prince Brat scornfully. "Didn't I tell you who I was? Bow low, you fools, and be off!"

But the two men neither bowed nor fled. Hold-Your-Nose Billy threw a bushy-eyed glance at his fellow outlaw.

"Cutwater, what do you reckon a genuine prince on the hoof is worth?"

"His weight in gold at least, Billy."

I was right. The villians are going to demand a ransom for their release.

(She continues reading)

Wisps of fog clung like tattered rags to the trees, and then the forest cleared. But so thick were the pines that the morning sun barely touched the ground.

Hold-Your-Nose Billy pushed aside a low branch, revealing a rickety timbered hut with a moldy thatched roof.

"There's our castle, Your Young Majesty," he said, chuckling. "Accept our hospitality! I hope you won't mind sleeping on the floor."

The floor was hard-packed earth. Braided garlic bulbs hung like knotted ropes from the rafters.

The description of their hut reminds me of the social studies lesson about the same kind of houses that the poor people lived in during the middle ages.

(Stacie resumes reading)

> *"I'm hungry," announced Prince Brat.*
>
> *"And feast you will," said Hold-Your-Nose Billy. "Cutwater, serve 'em up our finest bread and herring."*
>
> *Jemmy had made many a meal on bread and herring, when he was in luck, and felt hungry enough to ask for seconds.*
>
> *Prince Brat bared his teeth. "I'd sooner eat mud!" He reached for the wicker basket, but Cutwater snatched it back.*

Prince Brat probably packed good food in the basket before he left the castle.

(She resumes reading)

> *"What we got here?" muttered the bone-thin man, and thew back the lid. "Roll your eyes at this, Billy! Meat pies, looks like, and fruit tarts—and a brace of roast pheasant! We'll eat like kings!"*
>
> *"Hands off—that's mine!" the prince cried out.*
>
> *"Was yours," yapped Cutwater.*
>
> *Lawks! Jemmy thought. Hadn't the prince run away in royal style! He had even brought a China plate, a silver spoon, and a silver knife for himself.*

Jemmy and Prince Brat are so different. Prince Brat only thinks of himself. I predict that Jemmy will figure out a way for the two of them to escape.

As Stacie read and thought out loud, Andrea filled out the checklist, marking the strategies that Stacie was using.

The first time or two that my students use this technique, I find that some students have trouble remembering to verbalize their thoughts. To help them get the hang of it, I stop them at certain points in the text and ask questions such as: Is the story making sense? Can you retell what you have read? What do you picture in your mind after reading that? What do you think will happen next? I encourage them to look at the checklist for the strategies they need to verbalize. I also encourage the listeners to ask the readers questions and give them reminders.

At the end of the period I have the class discuss how thinking out loud helped them understand what they read. Most students say the activity was fun, and agree that the technique helped them concentrate on their reading and remember more of what they read. Students keep the checklist, and I encourage them to use it while they practice thinking out loud as they read for pleasure.

Follow-Up Activities

REPEAT THE LESSON

The next day I model the activity again, and have the students check the strategies I use on the checklist. They also practice with partners again.

Throughout the year I model the procedure and have students practice with different types of reading materials, including text books, nonfiction, and periodicals. In order for students to be able to use these strategies—especially those who are having difficulty comprehending—they need to experience them often.

READING A WEEKLY PERIODICAL

I have found the metacognition technique to be an effective method for reading a weekly newspaper such as *Scholastic News*. Having students verbalize their thoughts as they read aids them in understanding how to read nonfiction. I also find that students are more likely to use context clues in figuring out new vocabulary when they think out loud as they read. The format of the periodical also encourages students to retell what they have read more frequently. If they can't retell a section to their partners, they reread it, which improves their comprehension. When they finish reading their current-events newspaper, I have them write a response and/or a summary in their reading journals about at least one of the major articles.

READING A TEXTBOOK

You can adapt these strategies when teaching students how to get the most out of a textbook. For example, I often ask students to use the strategy of *surveying the lesson* before reading it by looking at the pictures, maps, graphs, headings, questions, and summaries. I guide students to use the headings to ask questions and look for answers as they read. I model a think-aloud as I read a textbook assignment, then give them a chance to work with a partner to do the same.

INDEPENDENT READING

Thinking out loud is not the ultimate goal for students, of course. The goal is to have children internalize these strategies so that they will use them intuitively as they read on their own. Often at the beginning of our silent reading period, I remind students to use the strategies that good readers use.

Evaluation

READING CONFERENCE

After the first two practice sessions with peers, I have each student meet with me to read and think out loud. I look for the prior knowledge they bring to the text, and note how they relate that to what they are reading. I also note the other strategies they use, give assistance to advance their understanding, and write anecdotal notes, which I refer to when forming small groups to brush up on skills and strategies. Through these conferences, I praise students for employing specific reading strategies. For example, I might say, "I like the way you went back and reread those sentences because they didn't make sense to you. I also noticed that you made predictions based on what you had already read. That's what good readers do!" Specific praise helps students to think about the strategies they are applying when they read.

PAIRED READING

As I sit with a pair of students who are practicing thinking out loud, I note the strategies they use and praise them when they apply specific reading strategies. Students can use the strategies checklist as a self-assessment tool. I can also refer to that checklist when evaluating and planning future lessons.

LEARNING LOG

Periodically, I ask students to write an explanation of what they know about a particular strategy—such as context clues—and how they use it. If you use learning logs in your classroom, they are a natural place

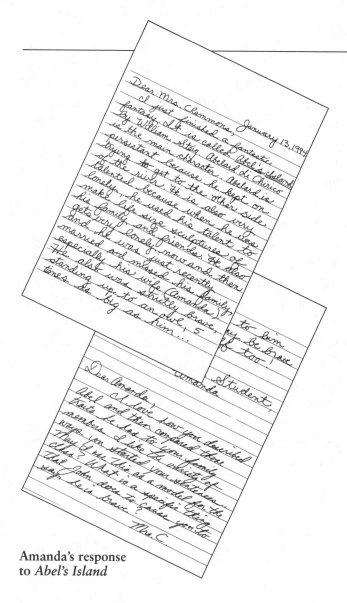

Amanda's response
to *Abel's Island*

for this kind of reflection. These written reflections show me whether or not students really understand the process.

STORY MAPS

Asking students to create or complete story maps related to the literature they have read is a good way to assess their comprehension of the text. For more about story maps, I recommend *Graphic Organizers: Visual Strategies for Active Learners* by Karen Bromley (Scholastic Professional Books, 1994).

READING JOURNALS

Reading journals—in which students write their responses to the books they are reading—are another useful means of evaluating students' comprehension skills. I have the students choose entries periodically to self-evaluate and to include in their portfolios.

RETELLINGS

Retellings help students develop comprehension skills. I also can use them to check for recall of details and to assess vocabulary and language development.

BOOK TALKS

When a student discusses a book with a small group of his peers, I can observe and write anecdotal notes concerning his reading and language development. These book talks can be audiotaped periodically and included in the student's portfolio.

PORTFOLIOS

Portfolios are wonderful vehicles for assessing reading. They chronicle students' development in reading throughout the year, and house a rich array of artifacts—from written literature responses to book-talk tapes—from which students can write detailed self-evaluations.

In addition to evaluating past work, students can use the portfolios to help them define goals for improving. Often students will mention using particular reading strategies as a way to perfect their reading. For example, in November, Charles set the following goals for reading: "I will ask questions as I read and look for answers. When I come to new words, I won't give up. I will read the sentences and try to figure them out." In May, as Charles reflected on his portfolio and his progress in reading, he said, "When I read I don't forget. I use the strategies I learned in thinking out loud as I read. I ask questions, and when I stop reading I say in my head what I just read about. I like to read."

Through portfolios, the students become active participants in the evaluation process. They set goals for improvement, and select and evaluate samples of their work. These samples show attainment of their goals and also show achievement of other skills and strategies. You may want to read our other book, *Portfolios in the Classroom: A Teacher's Sourcebook* (Scholastic, 1993), for additional information on the use of portfolios.

CHAPTER 5

Taking Notes

OBJECTIVE   Students will write effective summary notes.

When you ask your students to take notes, do they copy full sentences and in some cases even full paragraphs from the text of the books they've read? The students I've taught surely did, which prompted me to develop this focus lesson on writing summary notes.

Students in all grade levels need to be taught note-taking skills. Without them, researching and writing reports will always be a painstaking endeavor. The trick is to teach these skills *when the students need them and not as an isolated lesson.* In short, each time students have a need to write notes, I model the note-taking process using the material they are studying at the time.

As with reading strategies, I have found the best way to model note-taking skills is to think out loud as I read from a text and write notes. In this way, students see how I decide the main idea and supporting details of a particular paragraph. I can use the same procedure whether I'm teaching students how to write summary notes from nonfiction trade books, reference books, videos, filmstrips, interviews, textbooks, or articles.

How I Do It

To prepare for the lesson, I select sample paragraphs from nonfiction books related to our current unit of study. I make transparencies of these paragraphs to use as I model note-taking. To ensure that all of my students can see the samples easily, I enlarge the paragraphs on a copy machine or retype them before making the transparencies.

SETTING THE STAGE

▲ ▲ ▲ ▲ ▲ ▲ ▲

Asking students what they already know about writing summary notes causes them to relate to their current knowledge and stimulates their interest in finding out more about note-taking.

▼ ▼ ▼ ▼ ▼ ▼ ▼

I begin the lesson by writing my objective on the chalkboard, "Today you will learn how to write summary notes." Clearly displaying the goal helps students who are visual learners—they not only hear the objective but they can read it—and helps all students stay focused on the lesson.

Next, I ask students what they already know about taking notes. Sometimes I find it necessary to prompt them with questions such as: What is a summary? What do you do when you take notes on a topic you are researching?

As students respond, I write their comments on chart paper.

> It's what the book is about.
>
> It's short.
>
> I write down what is important.

TIME TO MODEL

Now that the stage is set, it's time to model how to write notes in one's own words. During our Egypt unit, for example, I place the transparency on the overhead projector of the paragraph taken from the nonfiction book *Ancient Egypt* by George Hart (Knopf, 1990).

Linen, made from flax (plant fiber) provided clothing materials for everyone in ancient Egypt. The earliest picture of a loom in Egypt is on a pottery bowl dated to c. 3000 B.C. and flax was used for thousands of years after that. A pharaoh would have exceptionally fine linen; workers wore loincloths of coarser fabric. The Egyptians had clever ways of reducing wear on linen clothes—soldiers would cover the rear of their kilts with leather netting; domestic servants wore nets of cheap but colorful beads over their dresses. The basic courtier's kilt consisted of a linen cloth wrapped around the waist and secured by a knot, often elaborately tied. Cloaks gradually developed for use as overgarments. Women wore long, close-fitting dresses, often with beautifully pleated cloaks. There are still only vague ideas about how the Egyptians put pleats into their clothes—perhaps they used a board with a grooved surface. The number of pleats is probably exaggerated in many statues. The Egyptians learned the art of dyeing their clothes in colorful patterns from the Middle East, but the technique was never widespread.

Ancient Egypt by George Hart (Knopf, New York; 1990)

▲ ▲ ▲ ▲ ▲ ▲ ▲

Throughout the school year— and throughout the curriculum— model the process of how you think as you read and take notes. The more you model by thinking aloud, the easier it is for students to understand the idea.

▼ ▼ ▼ ▼ ▼ ▼ ▼

After reading aloud the paragraph to my students, I go back to the beginning and say aloud what I'm thinking as I reread each sentence. For example, I begin by saying: "This sentence is about clothing in ancient Egypt," and "This sentence mentions a loom used in weaving cloth." I read aloud the third sentence and say, "This sentence tells the kind of cloth worn by pharaohs and workers." I continue in this manner until I reach the end of the paragraph. Then I think aloud, "Since all of the sentences in this paragraph are about clothing in ancient Egypt, the topic of the paragraph is the clothing of ancient Egypt. Therefore, I will write the topic—Clothing of Ancient Egypt—at the top of my note-taking sheet."

Next, I explain to students that I will find the important ideas or details that give information about the topic of the paragraph. As I reread the paragraph slowly, I underline the key phrases. I explain to students that the words I am underlining are important details about the clothing of ancient Egypt. Again, I think aloud and explain why I think certain words are important and why others are not. For example, I might say: "*Flax, 3000 B.C., pharaoh,* and *fine linen* are important words to remember because they refer directly to ancient clothing, but words like *provided, the pottery bowl,* and *clever* do not refer directly to ancient clothing."

Linen, made from flax (plant fiber) provided clothing materials for everyone in ancient Egypt. The earliest picture of a loom in Egypt is on a pottery bowl dated to c. 3000 B.C. and flax was used for thousands of years after that. A pharaoh would have exceptionally fine linen; workers wore loincloths of coarser fabric. The Egyptians had clever ways of reducing wear on linen clothes—soldiers would cover the rear of their kilts with leather netting; domestic servants wore nets of cheap but colorful beads over their dresses. The basic courtier's kilt consisted of a linen cloth wrapped around the waist and secured by a knot, often elaborately tied. Cloaks gradually developed for use as overgarments. Women wore long, close-fitting dresses, often with beautifully pleated cloaks. There are still only vague ideas about how the Egyptians put pleats into their clothes—perhaps they used a board with a grooved surface. The number of pleats

---

On the chart paper where I listed the topic, "Clothing of Ancient Egypt," I jot down the supporting details and emphasize that I'm putting the ideas in my own words. Students compare what I am writing to what is written in the paragraph and notice that my notes are not the same words as the author's:

Clothing of Ancient Egypt

◆ linen woven from flax as early as 3000 B.C.
◆ pharaohs' clothes of excellent linen
◆ workers' clothes of rough cloth
◆ soldiers' clothes protected with leather nets
◆ servants' dresses protected by beads
◆ courtiers' linen kilts tied at waist
◆ women had long dresses and pleated cloaks

More Note-Taking Experiences

In the next step of the lesson, I put another paragraph from *Ancient Egypt* on the overhead projector and read it aloud. I invite students to help me discover the passage's topic and the supporting ideas, encouraging them to listen carefully and to think about each sentence. We discuss what all of the sentences are about, and when students have agreed on the topic of the paragraph, I write it as a heading on a sheet of chart paper. As I reread each sentence in the paragraph, I invite students to underline the key words or phrases on the transparency.

Animals in the Nile Valley

Desert animals
    lions, bulls, antelope, gazelles, hyenas, jackals

River animals
    pintail ducks, cormorants, pelicans, hoopes, crocodiles, hippos

Animal pictures in hieroglyphics

To help stress the importance of writing summary notes in one's own words, I turn off the overhead projector and have each student turn to a buddy next to him or her and orally summarize the paragraph. When they finish, I turn on the projector and have them refer to the underlined words and phrases on the transparency. I then have them list the important details underneath the topic on the chart paper.

Next, I bring out the chart on which students listed everything they knew about note-taking. I ask them what guidelines they would add? Together, students contribute ideas and write them on the chart paper, in their own language. Giving them the responsibility of revising the guidelines really helps them understand the concept. However, if students leave out an important step in the note-taking process, I'll ask them leading questions until the guidelines are complete. I might ask: How do you select the topic of the paragraph? Or, What do you think about as you read the sentences of the paragraph?

I always post this chart in my classroom for students to refer to when they are researching topics. We also add ideas to it as they learn other note-taking strategies.

Note-Taking Guidelines

What I Know About Note-Taking

- It's what the book is about.
- It is short.
- I write down what is important.
- I use my own words, not the author's words.
- I reread the paragraph and write the topic.
- I write the important ideas that tell about the topic.
- I make sure my notes are organized by topic.
- I do not copy the author's sentences.

WORKING TOGETHER

Students work in small groups to practice the skill of writing summary notes. To save time, I usually assign students to groups of two or three. With a large sheet of paper and a copy of another paragraph about Egypt, each group goes through the note-taking process. They read the paragraph and then discuss the idea of each sentence. When the group agrees on the topic of the paragraph, one student in each group

writes it on the paper. Next, they underline the key words or ideas before rewriting them in their own words. I move from group to group, giving assistance as needed and specific praise. I might say, "Daniel, I like how you explained the process you used in deciding the topic of the paragraph." As my students work and share, I observe their needs. Later I regroup those students with similar needs and reteach.

When most of the groups are finished, I call the whole class together and ask a few groups to share their notes. After each group shares, I try to get all of the students to interact by having them refer to the class chart on note-taking and asking them such questions as: Did the group identify the topic of the paragraph? Did they list the important ideas that support the topic? Are the phrases or sentences written in their own words?

REINFORCING THE SKILL

I have students write what they have learned about note-taking in their learning logs. Students also use the responses in the learning logs to ask me questions or tell me what they do not understand. The learning log responses help me identify the students who need additional assistance.

STUDENTS' SUMMARY NOTES

The students who understand the note-taking process can now work independently to read and write notes on the topics of research they have chosen. I bring together the students who are having difficulty and work with them in a small group. I use material from their research topics to reteach the needed skills.

When I present note-taking strategies to my students in meaningful contexts rather than in isolated skill lessons, they more easily integrate note-taking into their daily classroom work. I keep the student-generated Note-Taking Guidelines chart posted in the classroom for easy reference. I model the process periodically, too, to keep it fresh in students' minds. Before I expect them to take notes from other sources, such as a video or an interview, I first model how to do it.

Khufu
- lived 2,600 B.C.
- famous because of tomb
- He wasn't found in tomb
- Mother was found near tomb.
- Jewelry and furniture was found in tomb
- Must have been powerful if people built such a large tomb

Monica's notes

Follow-Up Activities

WRITTEN REPORTS

My students practice note-taking skills in meaningful situations. When they research a topic, they use these skills to gather and organize the information and write a report.

DATA-RETRIEVAL CHARTS

Another way to use note-taking is to develop a large class data-retrieval chart. The students write notes on cards and place them on the class chart. My students choose their own areas to research, but they all share the information placed on the data-retrieval chart. The chart is a group effort (see the mini-lesson, Data-Retrieval Chart: A Graphic Organizer, on page 69).

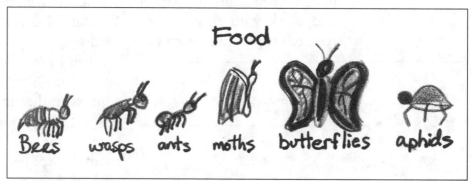

Notes about the praying mantis on the class data-retrieval chart

OTHER WAYS TO SHARE NOTES

I like to have students brainstorm a list of ways they can share their research with others. Knowing they will share their new knowledge motivates them to research thoroughly and take detailed notes. Students may show what they know by writing news shows, creating puppet shows and skits, and writing articles for school magazines and newspapers.

Evaluation

OBSERVATION AND ANECDOTAL NOTES

While I observe students working, I jot down anecdotal records, noting skills students have mastered, as well as those on which they need to work.

STUDENT REFLECTIONS

After we have studied a topic, I ask students to use their notes to help them reflect on what they've learned in their learning logs. The notes help students organize their ideas.

CONFERENCES

Often I will have a student bring her notes to a conference so we can discuss them together. I ask the student to explain the process she used to write the notes. Sometimes I have the student use her notes to discuss the topic of research with me.

STUDENT EVALUATIONS

When students have finished their research projects, they can write self-evaluations explaining what they have learned and what the projects demonstrate they can do. They can also set goals for self-improvement.

CHAPTER 6

Writing Paragraphs from Summary Notes

OBJECTIVE

Students will use summary notes to write reports.

Amy's Notes

Building Pyramids in Ancient Egypt
  Skilled Workers
    · Architects
    · Planners
    · Sculptors
        · Statues
        · Carvings
    · Painters
        · Decorated walls
    · Quarry men
    · Masons
        · Worked with stone
  Unskilled Workers
    · Farmers
    · Prisoners
    · People who owed labor tax

Amy's Paragraph

It took many people to build a pyramid. Several people who worked on the pyramids were greatly skilled like architects, planners, sculptors, painters, quarry men, and masons. Masons were people who were skilled at working with stone. There were other workers too who were not skilled, like farmers, prisoners, and people owing labor tax. When the structure was finished, the painters would decorate the walls, and the sculptors would sculpt statues and carve things.

Amy used several sources to research how the ancient Egyptians built pyramids. She used the summary notes that she had written under topical headings such as *workers, tools, quarry,* and *blocks* to help her draft the paragraphs of her report.

When students are taking summary notes for the purpose of writing a report, I model the process of writing a paragraph beforehand. We cannot over teach this process—students need to see how we decide on the topic sentence and supporting sentences many times before they truly understand the concept.

How I Do It

To prepare for this lesson, I locate the paragraphs I want to use as examples. There are many wonderful nonfiction books available for modeling good paragraph writing. However, I always try to use paragraphs that relate to the topic we're studying.

SETTING THE STAGE

We were studying Egypt at the time of this lesson; and since the students are usually intrigued by mummies, I chose the following paragraph to read aloud to the class.

> *What is a mummy, and why do we find mummies so fascinating? We've all heard of old-time horror movies with names like* The Mummy's Hand, The Mummy's Ghost, *and* The Mummy's Tomb. *And then there is "the mummy's curse." Even today there are people who believe that anyone who has ever gone near a mummy will meet with sudden misfortune.*
>
> *Mummies, Tombs, and Treasure*
> by Lila Perl (Clarion Books, 1987)

This paragraph always stimulates a lively discussion. After talking for a while, I reread the paragraph aloud. I have students tell me what they already know about writing a coherent paragraph, and ask them whether they think the one I just read is an effective paragraph. I write their ideas on chart paper.

DIEGO: A paragraph should be about one topic, and this paragraph is all about mummies.

MRS. C: It certainly is about mummies. What else do you know about paragraphs, and is the paragraph I just read to you a good example?

NICOLE: It has a topic sentence. The first sentence is a question, and it is the topic sentence.

I continue the discussion until the ideas are exhausted. Then I put another paragraph on the overhead projector.

Yet a mummy is nothing more than a dead body, either human or animal. Perhaps the reason mummies fill some of us with fear and fire up our imaginations is that they are so lifelike. Many Egyptian mummies are thousands of years old. But they still have their hair, their fingernails and toenails, and even their eyelashes. Their flesh and their features are well preserved. In looking at photographs taken when these mummies were discovered, in recent times, we can tell them apart and recognize their faces.

Mummies, Tombs, and Treasure

We discuss the paragraph and talk about how it measures up to what we know about effective paragraphs. As students talk, I continue to chart their ideas.

An Effective Paragraph . . .

- has one topic.
- has a topic sentence.
- has supporting sentences which give details or facts about the topic.
- has vivid words.
- does not have run-on sentences.
- has sentences that make sense and stick to the topic.
- has sentences that are in an order that make sense.

MODELING PARAGRAPH-WRITING

I begin this part of the lesson by writing our objective on the chalkboard, "Today you will use your summary notes to write the paragraphs of your report." I tell students that I will use their standards for an effective paragraph as I draft a paragraph.

Next, I display the notes on the Clothing of Ancient Egypt that I wrote in a previous lesson so everyone can see.

Clothing of Ancient Egypt

- ◆ linen woven from flax as early as 3000 B.C.
- ◆ pharaohs' clothes of excellent linen
- ◆ workers' clothes of rough cloth
- ◆ soldiers' clothes protected with leather nets
- ◆ servants' dresses protected by beads
- ◆ courtiers' linen kilts tied at waist
- ◆ women had long dresses and pleated cloaks

I read aloud the notes, and then use the think-aloud method, saying, "Since each sentence states something about the clothing, the topic of the paragraph I'm going to write is the clothing of ancient Egypt. I want the first sentence to be the topic sentence—which states the main idea of my paragraph. So I'll write *The ancient Egyptians used linen to make their clothes.*"

I then write the sentence on the chart paper for students to see, and continue to think aloud: "Now I will refer to my notes for the details I need to use in the supporting sentences which will explain this topic sentence."

I continue to write and read aloud the sentences.

> "As early as 3000 B.C., they wove the cloth from a plant called flax. The best linen was used in the pharaohs' clothes, while that in the workers' clothes was of a rough texture. To extend the wear of their clothes, soldiers put leather netting over the backs of their kilts, and servants covered their dresses with nets made of beads. A courtier tied a piece of linen around his waist for his kilt. Long dresses were worn by the women, and they often placed pleated cloaks over them. Linen was the fabric used in all ancient Egyptian clothing."

MODELING REVISION

After I finish writing the first draft, I show students how I revise it, thinking aloud as I make changes. Students refer to their criteria for

an effective paragraph to help me revise mine. I reread the entire paragraph and then get them involved in revising. I ask them:

- to state the topic and the main idea of the paragraph,
- to list the details in the other sentences that support the main idea, and
- to determine if I used enough details to explain the main idea.

I often ask my students to reread and revise their writing, so it is important that I model the process.

To get them to further analyze the composition of the paragraph, I pose these questions.

- Do the sentences in the paragraph stick to the topic and make sense?
- Is it organized in the correct order?

To get them to analyze the style of the paragraph, I ask them:

- to find evidence of vivid vocabulary (I always use the thesaurus when I model writing) and
- to find evidence of specific vocabulary.

Questions that assist the students further are:

- Do I have any run-on sentences?
- Are my sentences choppy?
- What are some interesting words or ways that I started my sentences? Can I improve them?

Cues for sentence formation include:

   ◆ Did I or how did I expand my sentences?

   ◆ Are they all complete sentences?

   ◆ Are the words in the correct order?

We quickly edit the mechanics of writing.

   ◆ Are the words spelled correctly?

   ◆ Are the words capitalized correctly?

   ◆ Is the paragraph indented?

   ◆ Is the punctuation used correctly?

In word usage we check that:

   ◆ the plurals, possessives, adverbs, and verb tenses are correct;

   ◆ subjects and verbs, as well as the pronouns and their antecedents, agree;

   ◆ the vocabulary used is accurate; and

   ◆ the paragraph sounds right as they read it.

REVISING THE STANDARDS CHART

When my students and I finish revising and editing the paragraph, I ask if there are any more guidelines for writing paragraphs that we need to add to the chart. After adding their suggestions to the chart, I post it in the classroom for the students to use as they write and revise their drafts.

An Effective Paragraph . . .

   ◆ has one topic.

   ◆ has a topic sentence.

   ◆ has supporting sentences which give details or facts about the topic.

   ◆ has vivid words.

   ◆ does not have run-on sentences.

   ◆ has sentences that make sense and stick to the topic.

   ◆ has sentences that are in an order that makes sense.

   ◆ has sentences that begin in different ways.

   ◆ is made up of sentences that flow.

   ◆ needs to be revised and edited.

STUDENTS WRITE THEIR DRAFTS

Now it is time for students to use their summary notes that they have written on their chosen topics to write the first draft of a paragraph. If a student has researched and taken notes on several facets of a topic, I encourage him to write several paragraphs.

WRITING CONFERENCES AND REVISION

After students revise their first drafts, they confer with a peer. One of the authors reads his draft, and his partner tells him what she likes about the piece of writing. Then they use ideas on the Effective Paragraph chart to guide their discussion. They identify the main idea of the paragraph and its supporting details. I encourage them to ask each other questions when they don't understand something in their partner's paragraph. They discuss whether or not there are sufficient details to support the main idea and whether or not all of the sentences stick to the topic. They may also offer each other suggestions about sentence structure and style. After following the same procedure with the other author's draft, the two students revise accordingly.

The students may also confer with a small group of peers or with me. Sometimes I am a member of the small group conference. Students discuss their paragraphs in these group conferences or with me in the same way they did when they conferred with a partner earlier. They use suggestions made in these conferences to continue to revise their drafts. In addition to the class chart, I also provide them with a list of writing criteria to use as they edit their papers. This is a great help to those students who have difficulty transferring information from a chart.

▲ ▲ ▲ ▲ ▲ ▲ ▲

It is necessary to model the revision process as the students work through their drafts. Many students think one revision is enough. Frequently I use a student-written paragraph that I have saved from a previous class as my model for revising.

▼ ▼ ▼ ▼ ▼ ▼ ▼

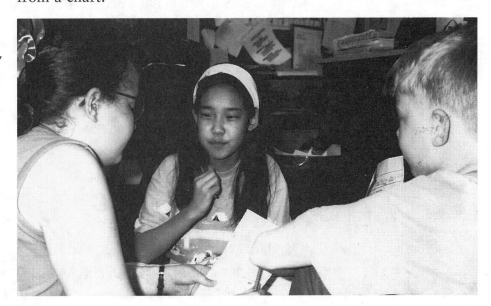

REVISING CHECKLIST

As a Writer, Did I ...

- ◆ refer to my notes and develop my ideas into paragraphs?
- ◆ revise my drafts?
- ◆ confer with others in writing conferences?
- ◆ continue to revise after participating in writing conferences?
- ◆ use a dictionary and thesaurus to check and extend my vocabulary?
- ◆ edit my work so that others can read it?
- ◆ correct spelling, punctuation, and grammatical errors?

Does My Writing Show ...

- ◆ paragraphs in which each is built around a main idea?
- ◆ the use of details and examples in sentences that support the main idea in each paragraph?
- ◆ paragraphs that make sense?
- ◆ complete sentences?
- ◆ a variety of sentence types that flow?
- ◆ appropriate vocabulary?
- ◆ consistent use of correct tense?
- ◆ correct spelling?
- ◆ correct punctuation?
- ◆ agreement between subject and verb?
- ◆ agreement between pronoun and antecedent?

AMANDA'S PARAGRAPH

This is one of Amanda's enlightening paragraphs that she drafted from her notes. She revised it several times using the criteria chart that she and her peers developed.

Draft 2

~~What Is A Mummy~~

What is a mummy? A mummy is a corspe that is dried out so it ~~won't~~ will not rot.
Long ago ~~they~~ the ancient egyptians mummified naturally. The corspe was buried ∧ in the ground. Then the burning sand dried out the body. ~~It~~ The corspe turned ~~as hard as rock or a fossil~~ into the textures like a fossil. The word mummy comes from mummiya ~~it~~ which means embalmed body. Embalmed means to protect a body from decaying.

PUBLISHING STUDENTS' REPORTS

What is a mummy? A mummy is a corpse that is dried out so it will not rot. Long ago the ancient Egyptians mummified naturally. The corpse was buried in the ground, and the burning sand dried out the body. The corpse turned into textures like a fossil. The word mummy comes from mumiya which means embalmed body. Embalmed means to protect a body from decaying.

After students finish revising and editing, they publish their reports. Some choose to publish them in large booklets in which they can illustrate many of their ideas. Others prefer to type their final copies on the computer.

Follow-Up Activities

SHARING THE REPORTS

When all students finish their reports, they share them with one another, sometimes as a whole class and other times in small groups. The students now become the teachers, and it is their responsibility to make the reports interesting. Before the sharing begins, we brainstorm different ways they can present their material. They suggested

- dressing the part,
- using props such as pyramids and tools,
- presenting the report as a skit,
- drawing pictures to go with the report, and
- presenting the information with enthusiasm as a television news report.

I encourage students to take notes during their classmates' presentations, jotting down what they consider to be the important information and any questions they have. I always encourage students to ask each other questions at the conclusion of a presentation, to clear up misunderstandings and to test the knowledge of everyone. The presenter must know the material thoroughly in order to answer questions, and the listener must stay tuned into the report in order to ask questions.

▲ ▲ ▲ ▲ ▲ ▲ ▲
Sharing research and written reports in a variety of ways—from dramatic monologues to scale-models— accommodates students' various learning styles and increases the achievement of all of the learners.
▼ ▼ ▼ ▼ ▼ ▼ ▼

Evaluation

TEACHER EVALUATION

It is important to evaluate the students during the entire writing process. Therefore, as I observe and help my students, I write anecdotal notes about how each is using the writing process, as well as what the writing shows.

> Steven used the thesaurus + selected appropriate synonyms Paragraph has gd. beginning but contains a run-on sentence. Misspelled pyramid.

Not only do I use the anecdotal notes in describing the student's achievement, I also use them for planning future lessons based on the students' needs. I look for areas of need in my notes and group the students appropriately for the instruction necessary for them to grow as writers.

As I confer with each student, I also learn how they made decisions about the development of their writing. The skills I am looking for and noting are similar to those I stressed as I modeled and revised my paragraph. Sometimes I use a checklist of criteria like the one I give the students, as we revise a piece of writing.

PEER WRITING CONFERENCES

Pairing students for peer writing conferences provides opportunities for students to comment on each other's writing. This helps young writers develop peer writing standards, which motivates their improvement.

STUDENT SELF-EVALUATION

▲ ▲ ▲ ▲ ▲ ▲ ▲

Building self-confidence is necessary in developing proficient writers.

▼ ▼ ▼ ▼ ▼ ▼ ▼

It is important for students to participate in the evaluation process. As they help me develop the standards for an effective paragraph, they are identifying the criteria of good writing. This process not only assists them in writing paragraphs, it also assists them in evaluating their own writing.

Usually with a piece of writing that has gone through all of the steps of the writing process—prewriting, drafting, revision, editing, publishing—I have students reflect on it and then write a response that states what the piece demonstrates they can do in writing. Not only does this make them aware of the criteria of good writing that they are able to use, it also builds self-esteem.

CLASSROOM MANAGEMENT TIP

Some of my students have trouble staying on task during all of the steps of the writing process. To assist them with their self-discipline, I have them make evaluation charts that they keep in their writing folders (left). Every day, at the end of writing workshop, students fill in the chart, noting what they have accomplished during the day and evaluating their work and/or behavior. Whenever they complete their writing project, they attach the evaluation chart to it. My students know that I include this in their over-all evaluation. I find that when the students evaluate their actions each day, they take more responsibility for their own learning.

Amy

Date	Piece of Writing	Accomplishment	Self Evaluation
3/1/94	How to build pyramids	I started on my book and put 4½ of my topics in it. I drew pictures for them too.	I accomplished a lot today. I am proud. I was able to stay on task
3/4/94	How to build pyramids	I finished the last 3½ topics of my book and started the coloring	I was able to stay on task I am very proud of myself
3/4/94	How to build pyramids	I finished coloring and proof reading my book. I labeled all my pictures that I color	I was able to stay on task and I got a lot done.
3/7/94	How to build pyramids poem	I started my poem and did 2 drafts and started my 3rd one.	I was able to stay on task. I am proud.
3/8/94	How to build pyramids poem	I finished a three paragraph poem and I started on another poems about pendulums.	I was able to stay on task and it payed off because I got I got a lot done.

My Evaluation of my writing

68

CHAPTER 7

Data-Retrieval Chart: A Graphic Organizer

OBJECTIVE Students will use a data-retrival chart to organize summary notes.

"When are we going to do another one of these charts?" my students often ask after completing a class data-retrieval chart. This type of graphic organizer is a wonderful technique to use to engage students in research throughout the content areas.

THE CHART'S BENEFITS

A data-retrieval chart helps students organize and learn information about a topic they are studying. Students can use them to categorize facts they summarize from several sources. The skills and strategies students develop as they create and use a chart include reading, thinking, summarizing, comparing and contrasting information, drawing conclusions, analyzing, and making generalizations about the data.

In requiring students to categorize information and organize their thoughts, the charts strengthen students' reading skills and expository writing skills.

How I Do It

I have used data-retrieval charts as a technique in teaching units in the content areas since I read about them in the *Elementary Writing Guide,* a resource published by the County School Board of Fairfax County, Virginia, in 1983. My students enjoy working in cooperative groups to complete class data-retrieval charts. I also have available desk-size blank charts for individual students to use during independent research. The way the students and I organize and develop a data-retrieval chart depends on its purpose and the content being studied.

DEVELOPING A CLASS CHART

1. I first choose a topic for students to investigate, such as insects, planets, explorers, American colonies, or life in the Middle Ages.

2. I decide on the research categories the cooperative groups will pursue, incorporating questions students have about the topic

with the curriculum objectives for the unit. For instance, for a study of insects, the students researched the following.

- ◆ Insect
- ◆ Life Cycle
- ◆ Food
- ◆ Habitat
- ◆ Importance of the Insect
- ◆ Anatomy
- ◆ Other Interesting Facts
- ◆ Sources Used

These categories can also be written in the form of questions.

3. I prepare a class data-retrieval chart using a 3-by-6-foot sheet of butcher paper, or any type of paper. I use a yardstick and a black marker to draw a grid, making as many columns as there are categories and as many rows as there are research topics. I laminate the chart so I can use it repeatedly. (We don't write on the chart; we tape our data to it.)

4. I cut out pieces of paper that are the same size as the blocks of the grid—4-by-6-inch pieces are ideal, as they allow enough room for students to add illustrations. I like to color-coordinate the rows. For example, the cards related to the monarch butterfly will be one color, while those about the dragonfly will be another color. This makes it easier for the students to use the chart.

5. I gather trade books, textbooks, encyclopedias, magazine articles, and related materials, as well as pencils, crayons, colored markers, tape, and glue.

"What We Already Know" is a useful category to include on your chart because it activates students' prior knowledge, and gets them revved up for researching.

Modeling the Process

I cannot stress enough how important it is to conduct lessons on writing summary notes before having the students create a data-retrieval chart. Please refer to Chapter 6 for suggestions in teaching this skill.

The first time I introduce the data-retrieval chart, I model how to complete a section of it. For example, in our study of insects, I ask students what they already know about the monarch. After recording their statements, I move to the next category and show students how to use the table of contents and index of a reference book to find the information they need.

| | | | Insects | | | | |
Insects.	Sources	Life Cycle	Food	Habitat	Importance	Anatomy	Other Interesting Facts
Monarch Butterfly	•The Monarch Butterfly by Judith P. Josephson. Mankato, MN: Crestwood House, 1988. •Amazing Insects by Laurence Mound. New York: Alfred Knopf, 1993.	Complete Metamorphosis •egg •larva •Pupa (chrysalis) •Adult butterfly	•egg •milkweed leaves •Nectar from flowers •Larva eats eggshell and milkweed leaves •Butterfly sucks nectar out of flowers with its proboscis	•North America •South America •Asia •Australia •Hawaiian Islands •parts of Europe •Flowers •Milkweed plants	•Caterpillar or larva eat only milkweed •As adult butterflies drink nectar, they aid in pollination (fertilization) of flowers.	•Head (eyes, antenne jaws here) •Thorax (legs + 4 wings here) •Abdomen	•Adult and caterpillar taste with their hair feel •Can fly up to 2000 miles to migrate •Can fly 80 miles in one day •Do not fly at night
Mantis	Mantises by Sylvia A. Johnson. Minneapolis: Lerner Publications Co., 1984. Amazing Insects by Laurence Mound. New York: Alfred A. Knopf, 1993.	•Incomplete Metamorphosis •egg •nymph •adult mantis •Nymphs grow by molting or shedding its exoskeleton. Adult body parts develop as it molts	Other insects	•many areas of the world •temperate climates •tropical climates	Eats many harmful insects	Head (4 wings + Thorax) On head are its eyes mostly and antennae Abdomen	•Big appetite •Cleans itself after eating •Females often eat their male mates •Smell with their antennae •Protected by its green color
Honeybees	Honeybees by Jane Lecht. National Geographic Society Library of Congress. 1973 •The World Book Encyclopedia Vol.2 Chicago: World Book, Inc. 1988.	Complete Metamorphosis •egg (laid in cells of honeycomb) •larva (fed honey & pollen by worker) •Pupa •adult	•honey •pollen	•Live together in a hive •On a near flowers •All over the world except North and South America	•Make honey which people eat •Help pollinate flowers which help plants to grow •Beeswax is used to make candles, crayons, lipstick, gum, and inks	•Head contains 5 eyes 2 antennae, and mouth parts •Thorax has 2 pairs of wings and 6 legs •Abdomen (contains the stinger)	•Loses stinger when it stings •Dies shortly after it loses its stinger •3 kinds of bees in the colony: queen, drones, and workers

A class data-retrieval chart on insects

Next I model how I read the text, summarize it, and record notes. I show them how to attach the paper containing the summary notes to the data-retrieval chart in the appropriate column, column by column, category by category. I model the process until I sense that the students have a good grasp of it.

Getting Students Started

I divide the class into groups of two or three to research a section of the class data-retrieval chart. Whenever possible, I match them to the area they are interested in researching. Together we discuss the guidelines for group work. The groups then meet and decide how they are going to approach their task and assign responsibilities to each member. I meet briefly with each group to make sure each student is involved and understands her or his responsibilities.

GATHERING THE INFORMATION

The students are now ready to find and digest the information pertinent to the question for which they are responsible. I encourage them to use the materials in the classroom and in the library to thoroughly investigate their topics. Children go about their work in a variety of ways—sometimes a group will choose to read aloud from a source and discuss the information before formulating the summary notes. Others will read and write summary notes with a buddy. Some students may contribute by illustrating an aspect of the research, while others track down the reference materials.

HELPING STUDENTS COMPLETE THE CHART

I move from group to group assisting students in various ways—helping them locate information, thinking of new sources, reading aloud key passages, and so on. Sometimes I reteach a group of students how to write summary notes.

When students finish writing and illustrating the summary notes, they attach the paper to the chart. They continue in this manner until the data-retrieval chart is complete.

INDIVIDUAL SUMMARIES

In addition to note-taking, the students need to summarize the information they record on the chart. Each group rereads their notes and writes a group summary of the information they recorded. Summary can be one of the headings on the data-retrieval chart, and they can

post their summaries under it. Or the summaries can be organized to create a class book on the main topic. Another method is to have each student independently write a summary of his group's notes in his learning log. Regardless of the method I choose, I first model the writing of a summary. Using the notes I wrote and placed on the data-retrieval chart when we started this activity, I write a summary of them for all of the class to see.

Follow-Up Activities

COMPARE AND CONTRAST

Using the notes on the data-retrieval chart the children can compare and contrast information. For example, I ask my students to compare their prior knowledge with the new data. I lead them in a discussion of how their misconceptions were clarified. Each group can also compare and contrast the information they learned with the information other groups gathered. I also find it valuable to have them compare and contrast the kinds of information found in various sources.

SHARING RESEARCH

I encourage groups to share their research. To avoid having the students just stand and read their summaries, I invite groups to teach the rest of the class the information they have learned. We brainstorm interesting ways they can do this, and I chart their suggestions. The groups decide on their method of presentation, and I allow them sufficient time to prepare for it. Here is a list of some of the activities the students especially enjoy creating.

Ways to Share Research

- skits
- plays
- readers' theater
- role-playing
- radio/television shows
- interviews
- debates
- magazines
- board games
- Venn diagrams
- bulletin board displays
- poems
- comic strips
- written reports
- songs/raps
- drawings
- puppet shows
- stories
- class books
- time lines
- videotapes
- murals

Allison wrote and presented this poem as part of her presentation about ancient Egyptian tools.

> **Egyptian Tools** *by allison*
>
> The Egyptian tools were made
> From anything at hand
> And they didn't use bulldozers,
> Or even rubber bands!
>
> There were flat tips there were
>   sharp tips,
> There were bronze and copper hooks,
> There were bows and arrows, ramps
>   and bricks,
> And hieroglyphic books.
>
> They made bricks from wooden molds,
> And weights for their nets.
> They made throwsticks and many others
> Such as writing pallets.
>
> The Egyptians thrived
> With no technology
> But wouldn't it be hard
> For just you and me!

I encourage students to listen carefully and take notes during their peer's presentations, and to be prepared to ask questions about anything they don't understand. The students really enjoy presenting their own research, as well as learning about the other topics in this manner. One of my students, Elliot, commented after several of the presentations, "Gosh, this is really fun!"

After the presentations, I have students use the notes they have taken to help them write an entry in their learning logs. The entry should explain the new information they have learned from the other groups.

Additional Class Data-Retrieval Charts

Since data-retrieval charts are especially helpful to students in organizing and learning information in the content areas, class charts can be made for various units of study throughout the school year. Remember, though, that exciting charts depend on a

> *Spiders by Judy*
>
> ... The jumping spider can jump many times its own length. It also spins a thread to pull itself up after it is done hunting.
>
> The wolf spider moves at great speeds. Female wolf spiders carry their egg sacks on their backs.
>
> The trapdoor spider digs a burrow and builds a trap door. When an insect comes along, a trap door spider feels the vibrations and opens the door and catches the insect and drags it into its burrow.
>
> Common house spiders spin uneven webs, but orb weaving spiders decorate their webs. They make very fancy webs.
>
> Billions of spiders are helpful to trees! The spiders eat budworms and help prevent trees from dying. ...

A student's learning log entry

Jill writes notes.

rich array of resource books. There are many wonderful nonfiction books and innovative reference books available now that not only enhance our teaching, but also enhance student achievement. They can make an historical topic, a science lesson, or a skill that we teach come alive. Using trade books in addition to the textbook makes learning fun and helps children become critical readers. A good resource containing an excellent bibliography of children's nonfiction books is *Using Nonfiction Trade Books in the Elementary Classroom From Ants to Zeppelins*, Evelyn B. Freeman and Diane Goetz Person, editors (National Council of Teachers of English, Urbana, IL, 1992).

INDIVIDUAL DATA-RETRIEVAL CHARTS

After my students have had the experience of working in groups on data-retrieval charts, many of them are eager and able to use individual desk-size data-retrieval charts. After they have chosen a topic, they generate questions to go across the top of the chart. I show them how they can use headings in the nonfiction books to help them choose good questions to research about their topics, and they're off and running. Students find their completed charts to be extremely helpful frameworks for their written reports.

Lisa's individual data-retrieval chart

Sources	Sicknesses and Medicines	Distances Traveled	Wagon Trains	Food and Water	Interests	(Animals) Horses - Oxen	Indians	Chores	Deaths
Cassie's Journey Author - Publishing Company City published in copyright date Whole book	·quinine (Medicine) for the fever. ·citric acid for scurvy	·15-20 miles a day	·12 wagons ·"elephant" when you turn back home. ·Never want to be lost	·flour ·sugar ·rice ·bacon ·dried meat ·vegetables (dried) ·yeast ·vinegar ·wild plum and blackberry jail. ·pancakes or bread ·coffee ·mosquitoes got in food.	·Dolls ·moccasins	·4 oxen to pull wagon ·milk cow ·watchdog		·Cooking ·gather buffalo chips ·Water and food supplies ·Make fire and supper ·Put up tents	
Ency. "Overland Trails" *New Book of Knowledge* Vol. O p. 293-279 William J. Brampon Danbury, Conn.	·If a man got injured or sick in any way there was no way to help him.	·50 miles of desert on the Santa Fe. ·300 miles through foothills. ·Climbs 200 miles in the Rockies.	·One wagon could carry 2 tons of goods. ·Many times they had to float or drag wagons across rivers so they could avoid steep cliffs. ·single wagons could easily be destroyed ·the trail was much like a highway with the cars and big trucks	·when they went thru deserts dust would sting their throats. Sometimes they thought that they would die of thirst. ·For 200 miles they ate only corn bread and coffee. ·In buffalo country they could kill buffalo and have fresh meat.		·1-12 mules or oxen pulled every wagon. ·mules had to be caught and shoed at post, harassed by the muleskinners. ·Men rode horses to watch for trouble.	·They could easily destroy and kill single families and wagons. ·Ambushing Whites.	·Each man had to take turns being post guards at night.	·Rattle snake bites. ·Falling out of wagon ·Fever
Wagons over the Mountains by Edith McCall Childrens Press Inc. 1961 21-78			·Riding on the Rocky Mountains was so rough most people packed everything on mules and left their wagon behind. ·Wagons had to be taken apart to cross rivers and climb mountains.	·Dry grass and buffalo chips were burned for fires to cook on.	·mules ·furs ·buffalo skins ·silver ·gold ·silver dollars	·6-8 mules or oxen to a wagon. ·4 horses ·6 mules	·didn't know how to use animals used travois to pull and take things.		

USING DATA-RETRIEVAL CHARTS FOR GENRE STUDIES

I also use a data-retrieval chart when my students are studying a particular type of literature, such as mysteries, fantasies, or folktales. It is effective in comparing and contrasting books in a particular genre. I construct a large class data-retrieval chart in the same way that I described earlier. I usually write the titles of the books we're reading along the side of the chart, and write the literary elements across the top.

During our study of literary fantasy, I divide my class into five groups. Each group reads a different novel:

- *The Trumpet of the Swan* by E. B. White (HarperCollins, 1942)
- *Charlotte's Web* by E. B. White (HarperCollins, 1952)
- *A Wrinkle in Time* by Madeleine L'Engle (Dell, 1962)
- *Abel's Island* by William Steig (Farrar/Straus/Giroux, 1976)
- *The Lion, The Witch, and the Wardrobe* by C. S. Lewis (Collier, 1950)

During this same period of time I read aloud another fantasy, *Pigs Might Fly* by Dick King-Smith (Scholastic, 1980). I use it to teach mini-lessons about literary fantasy and literature in general. We also compare it to the classic fantasies they are reading.

As students read and discuss their books in their groups, they also construct a class data-retrieval chart entitled Literary Fantasy. The categories we write across the top of the chart are based on the elements of literature we are studying: Title and Author, Setting, Characters and their Traits, How the Characters Handled their Various Problems, Personification, Main Events in the Order They Happened, and Theme(s). I find that the students are more actively involved in discussing these elements of their novel because they know they have to write about them on the data-retrieval chart. As they write the information for the categories, they interact with each other, discussing the topics even more thoroughly. Some students illustrate the information their classmates write. When they finish, they summarize their novels in their Literature Response Journals.

These literature charts have a great effect on students' reading habits. Children are often motivated to read the novels other groups have read. Not only are the students growing in their reading skills, but they are also developing as critical readers and thinkers.

We construct similar data-retrieval charts as we study folktales and mysteries. This is also a good technique to use when studying the writing style of a particular author. The students enjoy creating skits and plays as methods of sharing the information on the charts.

Evaluation

STUDENT EVALUATION

As a closure, I have the students come together at the end of each class period. The groups report on their accomplishments. They also discuss any problems they have and how they plan to solve them.

At the end of the unit of study, students write an evaluation stating what they have learned, as well as noting the skills and strategies they can now use. They also set goals based on their interests or based on skills and strategies they want to improve.

ANECDOTAL NOTES

Throughout the construction of a class data-retrieval chart, I observe students working and give assistance as needed. I write anecdotal notes about their participation as group members, as well as about the acquisition of skills and strategies. Based on these findings, I reteach needed skills or strategies to individuals or small groups of students.

I may find that I need to guide someone to less difficult reading materials or read aloud particular passages. In this ongoing evaluation, I am able to evaluate the learning process, as well as the final product.

CHAPTER 8

Revising Sentences

OBJECTIVE Students will recognize and write well-structured sentences and paragraphs.

After I've taught the parts of a sentence, there are always a number of students whose writings still contain run-on sentences, even after they have revised and edited. For some, it's a matter of becoming skilled at writing complete sentences. But for others, the run-on sentences signal that they are trying to expand their sentences by combining ideas into one sentence. These students are ready to be shown how to combine ideas skillfully.

I have found that teaching children how to identify and fix run-on sentences goes hand-in-hand with teaching them about flow—that is, how writers make sentences flow in a paragraph. After all, when they revise sentences within a paragraph, the flow of ideas changes. Revising writing is difficult for students. They need to be led through each step, and they must practice revision in all writing assignments.

How I Do It

PREPARATION

To prepare for the lesson, I select a paragraph from a work of non-fiction literature that is related to a unit we are studying. I copy the words from the paragraph end-to-end on strips of paper. However, I leave out all of the connecting words such as *both, also, besides, even, furthermore,* etc. I also write the ideas separately. That is, I do not use phrases to connect ideas. The paragraph, when reassembled by the students, will sound very choppy. This is necessary for the second part of the lesson. To make the sentences run on, I use no capital letters or end-of-sentence punctuation marks. Next, I tape the strips of paper together and fold them along the taped edges. (I learned this visual aid from Kay Houston, a teacher at our school.) I also make a copy of the original paragraph, enlarge it if necessary, and make a transparency of it.

For this activity I use a paragraph from Ken Teague's *Growing Up in Ancient China* (Troll Associates, 1994).

> Most people in ancient China were farmers the youngest children helped on the farm they would look after the work animal the work animal was a buffalo they took it to water they fed it the father would plow the children would guide the buffalo boys and girls helped grind the rice for cooking they helped feed the animals the older children took grain and vegetables to market they used wheelbarrows the main crop was rice in the south and center of China the main crop was wheat in the north.
>
> most people in ancient China were fa

Before the lesson, I also prepare a Venn diagram on a large piece of paper, and make copies of another well-written paragraph from the same source or from another book that is familiar to the students. Pairs of students will share these copies. I also draft and copy onto chart paper my own paragraph containing choppy sentences and run-on sentences. (See example on page 88.)

THE RUN-AWAY SENTENCE

To begin the lesson, I ask for a helper, and we proceed to unfold the long, run-away sentence. Of course, the students are amazed as they watch it unfurl. The dialogue begins something like this.

MRS. C: I have a very long sentence. Will someone read it for us? (After it is read) What is wrong with the sentence?

MICHAEL: It doesn't make sense!

PETER: There are no periods.

NICOLE: There are no capital letters.

KISHA: All the sentences run together.

I continue, "Yes, you have identified a run-away sentence. It includes several run-on sentences, and the objective of this lesson is to write paragraphs containing good sentence structure.

CORRECTING THE RUN-AWAY SENTENCE

First, I ask students to decide where capital letters and periods are needed. They use a marker to make these corrections. Students then cut the sentences apart and tape them to the wall or chalkboard in paragraph form. Even though they are choppy and parts are repetitive, they are complete sentences.

> Most people in ancient China were farmers. The youngest children helped on the farm. They would look after the work animal. The work animal was a buffalo. They took it to water. They fed it. The father would plow. The children would guide the buffalo. Boys and girls helped grind the rice for cooking. They helped feed the animals. The older children took grain and vegetables to market. They used wheelbarrows. The main crop was rice in the south and center of China. The main crop was wheat in the north.

Now I ask them to list the criteria for writing a complete sentence and I chart their ideas.

SENTENCES...

♦ begin with a capital letter.

♦ end with a period, question mark, or exclamation point.

♦ must make sense.

♦ do not run on and on.

♦ state a complete thought.

When I wrote the sentences, I purposely left out the connecting words and phrases, so that they would not flow or have rhythm. I want students to discover that they need to do more than just capitalize and punctuate correctly when they revise. The choppy-sounding paragraph is my lead into the next part of the lesson—making sentences flow.

As I ask students about the paragraph we have taped to the wall, they all agree that the sentences are complete. They also stick to one topic. However, students note that there is repetition, some of the sentences are choppy, and the paragraph does not sound great.

MAKING SENTENCES FLOW

I explain to students that we are going to read the paragraph the way it was written in the book and compare it to the way we wrote it on the chart paper. We will then analyze it to determine how the author wrote his ideas in complete sentences and connected them to make a good paragraph. I tell them that our discussion will help them revise their own work, because they will see that revision means more than putting capital letters and periods in place.

I place the transparency of the correctly written paragraph from *Growing up in Ancient China* on the overhead projector.

Life in the Country

Most people in ancient China were farmers. Even the youngest children helped on a farm. They would look after their work animal—a buffalo—by taking it to water and feeding it. Sometimes they would guide the buffalo when their father was plowing. Both boys and girls helped grind the rice for cooking. They also helped feed the animals, and older children took grain and vegetables to market in wheelbarrows. The main crops were rice in the south and center of China, and wheat in the north.

After reading aloud the paragraph, I ask students to compare and contrast this paragraph with the one which we edited by just adding capital letters and periods. I record their ideas on a Venn diagram.

I summarize the lesson by pointing out that authors do expand sentences by combining details in interesting ways. The ideas in three of the short sentences in our paragraph (*They looked after their work animal. The work animal was a buffalo. They took it to water and fed it.*) can be written as one good interesting sentence, as Ken Teague proved: *They would look after their work animal—a buffalo—by taking it to water and feeding it.* I point out that the author chose to

84

Our Edited Paragraph

Short sentences

Choppy sentences

Does not sound like a paragraph

Both

Topic: Life in the country in ancient China.

Main idea is most people in ancient China were farmers.

Have complete sentences.

K. Teague's Paragraph

Longer sentences.

Sounds good.

Uses words like *even* and *also*.

Ideas are combined to make a compound sentence.

use dashes to set off a buffalo because it meant the same thing as a work animal in the sentence. I also mention that commas could have been used instead of dashes to set off these words. I ask students to find other examples of where the author combined details. They contrast the next sentence—*Sometimes they would guide the buffalo when their father was plowing*—with the poorly written short sentences that we edited—*The father plowed. The children guided the buffalo.* I explain that by using the adverb *when*, the author was able to combine the ideas.

Some students' run-on sentences are compound sentences that they have not punctuated correctly, so I also explain that all writers, including themselves, sometimes want to write two sentences together because they are so closely related. But these sentences must be punctuated correctly so that they don't run-on. I guide them to the compound sentence, *They also helped feed the animals, and older children took grain and vegetables to market in wheelbarrows.* We discuss the two complete thoughts and how they are combined with the conjunction *and* and separated with the comma.

I praise them for finding the words, *even, also,* and *both* in Teague's paragraph and explain that words like these, as well as *besides, in addition, similarly, moreover, in each case, in fact, furthermore, to me, it seems that, in my view,* and *I notice that* are called connecting words because they connect details in a paragraph. They help to make the paragraph flow. (It is a good idea to write these connecting words on a chart that is accessible for the students to use as they revise and edit their writing.)

I explain that combining ideas into a single smoothly written sentence—and interspersing long sentences with shorter ones—gives one's writing flow and rhythm. I read aloud Teague's paragraph again, inviting children to listen for the sounds of good writing.

ELABORATING THE CRITERIA FOR GOOD SENTENCES

Next I refer to the chart containing the criteria for sentences that we developed earlier in the class and ask the students if there are additional ideas we need to add. As they make suggestions, I write them on the chart. The completed chart that I post in the classroom serves as a helpful reminder for my students as they write, revise, and evaluate their work.

Sentences...

- ◆ begin with a capital letter.
- ◆ end with a period, question mark, or exclamation point.
- ◆ must make sense.
- ◆ do not run on and on.
- ◆ state a complete thought.
- ◆ should not be choppy within a paragraph.
- ◆ need to flow or have rhythm in a paragraph.
- ◆ use connecting words like *also* and *both* to connect details.
- ◆ do not keep repeating the same words.
- ◆ have a comma before the conjunction that connects two complete thoughts in a compound sentence.

PAIRS OF STUDENTS ANALYZE SENTENCES

In the next step of this lesson I give pairs of students a copy of a different well-written paragraph and have them analyze the sentence structure. The paragraph can come from a book related to our unit of study; from the book I am reading aloud; or perhaps from a book that one of the students has read, retold, and discussed in class. For example, I might use a paragraph from a Chinese tale, "The Rainbow People," found in Laurence Yep's book, *The Rainbow People* (Harper-Collins, 1989).

> Even then, the rainbow people did not leave the fields. Instead, they went on working by the light they gave off. They stayed in the fields well into the night before they finally had their meal. However, they didn't go into the huts on one side of the valley. They just sat down in the fields.

I ask students to discuss with a partner the various ways the author wrote the sentences. After about five minutes, I have students share their discoveries. They mention such things as: The author combined ideas in well developed sentences and used connecting words and proper punctuation marks. By analyzing the sentences, the students gain ideas for ways they may be able to revise their own paragraphs containing run-on sentences.

MODELING REVISION

Now it's time to show students how I revise a paragraph that I have written. It contains poorly constructed sentences, as well as run-on sentences. As I revise it, I think aloud what I am doing.

MY FIRST DRAFT

> The Great Wall of China was built over two thousand years ago. It was built by China's first emperor he was Shih Huang Ti. He wanted the wall to keep out the invaders they were the warlike people who lived north of the border in central Asia. Laborers built the wall they connected shorter walls that had been built for defense by Chinese nobles years earlier. Ti ordered them to build watchtowers along the wall so that sentries could guard the fortification and send signals using smoke or fire to his capital. The wall extended four thousand miles across northern China. Parts of it are still standing today.

These are some of the thoughts I verbalize as I revise the paragraph on the chart paper. "I have completed my first draft of a paragraph about the Great Wall of China. As I read it aloud I will revise and edit it. *The Great Wall of China was built over two thousand years ago. It was built by China's first emperor he was Shih Huang Ti.* This sentence is a run-on sentence because I have two complete thoughts with no punctuation mark between them. I need to put a period after *emperor* and capitalize the *h*. However, I have repeated *was built*. I can write a better sentence by combining ideas in the first three sentences of this draft into one sentence. *The Great Wall of China was built over two thousand years ago by China's first emperor, Shih Huang Ti.*

I continue thinking aloud in this way as I revise the entire paragraph on the chart paper; students look on while I work. I cross out words, circle words, and use arrows to show where I want to move words, insert words, and so on. Because the first draft is messy, I rewrite it so the students can read it easily.

MY REVISED DRAFT

> The Great Wall of China was built over two thousand years ago by China's first emperor, Shih Huang Ti. He ordered the construction of the wall to keep out the invaders, or warlike people who lived north of the border in central Asia. Laborers constructed the wall by connecting shorter walls that had been built for defense years earlier by Chinese nobles. Ti also ordered the construction of watchtowers along the wall so that sentries could guard the fortification and send signals using smoke or fire to his capital. The defensive wall and watchtowers extended about four thousand miles across northern China, and parts of it are still standing today.

STUDENTS REVISE THEIR DRAFTS

I now give students time to rework their drafts that contain run-on sentences. I also encourage them to confer with partners after they have revised. As they read aloud their drafts to partners, they can hear how the language flows (or doesn't!) and discover additional ways they can revise their writing. The partners can also offer each other suggestions for revision.

CLOSURE

I like to close writing workshop each day by allowing three to five minutes for a few students to share something they have written that they especially like. It might be one of the paragraphs they revised, a single sentence they love, or a work-in-progress needing suggestions for improvement.

STUDENT SAMPLES

I make a practice of using my students' work as examples of good writing whenever possible. When I read a good piece that a student has written, I ask him for permission to use it as a model for the class. It may be a sentence, a paragraph, or an entire piece of writing. I make a copy and a transparency of it so that the class can see it as I or the author reads it aloud. Students are delighted to have their work highlighted in this manner, and all of them seem to pay very close attention when their peers' writings are being used in a lesson. Because student examples are effective in teaching writing, I save good examples to use in future years.

Evaluation

ANECDOTAL NOTES

As I read students' work, I write anecdotal notes about the progress they are making in developing good sentences. As I see the need for additional help, I reteach the necessary skills for writing good sentences to an individual or a group of students.

WRITING CONFERENCES

When I confer with individual students in writing conferences, I give plenty of specific praise and offer additional help when needed.

PORTFOLIOS

I can monitor a student's progress by comparing the various pieces of writing in his portfolio.

MASTERY CHECKLIST

On a writing mastery checklist, consistent evidence of good sentence structure can be noted.

STUDENT SELF-EVALUATION

I expect students to self-evaluate their writing. I have them reflect on their published pieces and write an evaluation explaining what the piece shows they can do. They may refer to the standards or criteria for good writing posted on the charts that they helped to develop in the various writing lessons.

Using a Thesaurus

OBJECTIVE — Students will use a thesaurus to improve their writing.

CREATING INTEREST

I begin this lesson by sharing an anonymous sample of student's work that contains overworked and tired words.

> *It was a cold day. I had to go outside to get the newspaper. I ran to get my coat.*

I then read a descriptive passage taken from a trade book. Some of my favorite passages, such as this one, come from *Dogsong* by Gary Paulsen (Scholastic, 1985).

> *Russel Susskit rolled out of the bunk and put his feet on the floor and listened in the darkness to the sounds of morning.*

It doesn't take the students long to discover that Gary Paulsen's passage vividly describes the scene whereas the first passage I read to them was, in the students' word, boring. I challenge students to find descriptive passages in the books that they are reading and to share them with each other.

After my students have had an opportunity to read aloud descriptive passages from their books, I ask them how they can make their own writing more descriptive. If they don't mention using the thesaurus, I always have one close at hand and show it to them. I tell them that with the help of a thesaurus writers have a world of colorful, unusual words at their fingertips.

How I Do It

First I make a transparency of a page from the thesaurus, as well as a transparency of student prose that lacks verve. If the thesaurus has small print, I enlarge it on the copy machine before I make the transparency. It is important that all students can read the text easily when it is displayed on the screen.

▲ ▲ ▲ ▲ ▲ ▲ ▲

Other books that I frequently refer to for descriptive passages are Hatchet *by Gary Paulsen,* The Trumpet of the Swan *and* Charlotte's Web *by E. B. White,* Abel's Island *by William Steig,* Bridge to Terabithia *by Katherine Paterson, and any of Roald Dahl's children's books. Of course, there are many other books with wonderful descriptive passages.*

▼ ▼ ▼ ▼ ▼ ▼ ▼

WHAT'S ON THE PAGE

Together, students and I examine the page from the thesaurus. I ask students to point out the different parts of the thesaurus and explain how they think the information is used. The first thing that a student usually notices is that the words are in alphabetical order. Our dialogue goes like this:

KATIE: The words are in alphabetical order.

MRS. L: Good observation. Come up to the projector, Katie and underline the words to show that they are in ABC order. Why do you suppose they are in alphabetical order?

JOSH: There are guide words like in a dictionary.

MRS. L: Another great discovery. Please come to the overhead and underline the guide words. Can you explain how to use guide words?

---

syn synonym(s)   *rel* related word(s)

ant antonym(s)   *con* contrasted word(s)

idiom idiomatic equivalent(s)

Webster's School Thesaurus

Meriam-Webster Inc.,

Springfield, MA, 1989

The interaction between the students and myself continues as we discover the key and the information included in the key.

We discuss the meaning of synonyms, antonyms, idioms, contrasting words, and related words. I encourage students to locate the synonyms on the transparency and to come to the overhead projector to highlight a few of them with a marker. Students then mark antonyms, contrasting words, and so on. We continue until all the parts of the page are discovered, discussed, and highlighted with a marker.

As soon as students understand the information that appears on a page of a thesaurus, I display the student sample that I selected.

> It was a cold day. I had to go outside to get the newspaper.
> I ran to get my coat.

I ask students to find synonyms or related words that they can substitute for the word *cold*. (I always make sure that the page I copied from the thesaurus has the word cold on it!) I invite different students to write the new sentences on chart paper or on the chalkboard.

It was a chilly day.
It was a freezing day.
It was a nippy day.

It is always fun to discover that not all the words are interchangeable. You have to look at the meaning and listen to it in a sentence to make certain it is a good synonym. Patrick had the class laughing as he tried out these two sentences.

It was an unemotional day.
It was an impersonal day.

Using the definitions found in the thesaurus, Patrick then explained to the class that in the first sentence *cold* means lacking cordiality and in the second sentence it means matter-of-fact. In the original sentence *cold* means marked by a deficiency of warmth; therefore, *chilly, freezing,* and *nippy* are good synonyms.

WORKING TOGETHER

Now I divide the class into groups and give each group a thesaurus and a large sheet of paper with a common, overused word written across the top. I give each group a different word, such as *went, said, nice, pretty, let, ran, ugly, good,* and *bad.* I select the overused words by looking through students' papers.

Now I ask each group to write a sentence using the overworked word and then to make a list of synonyms that can be substituted for their word. I rotate among the groups making certain they understand the assignment and that they stay on task. As a closure to this activity, one person from each group shares their list of words and hangs his group's chart where everyone can see it.

MEANINGFUL PRACTICE

So students can immediately put this lesson to use, I have them take out a piece of their own personal writing and skim through it to find

I ran to get my coat.
ran
hurried
rushed
hustled
scampered
raced
speeded

a tired, overused word. With the help of the thesaurus and the charts, students search for a synonym to substitute for their original word then share their original sentence and their new sentence.

I frequently hear students lament, "I can't find my word. It isn't in the thesaurus." Invariably it will be the past tense form of a verb, such as *ate*. A quick review lesson on the present tense of verbs usually solves the problem.

Follow-Up Activities

A PICTURE BOOK MAKES THE POINT CLEAR

Using Ruth Heller's books makes the students aware of the different parts of speech in an interesting way.

Ruth Heller's *Kites Sail High, A Book About Verbs* (Grosset & Dunlap, 1988) is a perfect extension of this mini-lesson. Before I read it aloud, I ask students to tell me everything they know about verbs, and I list their ideas. I then gather students as close to me as possible, so they can see the pictures in the book as I read aloud. We take time to discuss and enjoy both the text and the art. Afterward, I ask students what they now know about verbs. They are often very surprised to discover how much information about verbs they have learned from *Kites Sail High*.

MORE VERB VOYAGES

To widen students' vocabulary and to give them additional practice using the thesaurus, I again divide the class into small groups and arm them with a large sheet of paper. Each group chooses a common verb and writes it as the heading on the paper. Underneath it, they list other verbs they could possibly replace it with in a sentence. I ask one person from each group to write the group's common verb on the chalkboard. To speed up the process, I suggest common, overused verbs to the groups that are having difficulty.

At the conclusion of the lesson, the students share their lists and post them where all can

Some Common Verbs

do	want
see	tell
get	ask
like	start
know	say
walk	beat

see. This same lesson can be repeated by using Ruth Heller's books—*Many Luscious Lollipops, A Book About Adjectives* and *Up, Up and Away, A Book About Adverbs.*

It takes a lot of practice and encouragement to get students to feel comfortable with a thesaurus. To make this happen, I ask them to consult a class word chart or a thesaurus at least once for every paper they write. I'll find that at first students change words just for the sake of changing, or stubbornly think the first word they choose is perfect so why use the thesaurus! But with persistence and a good measure of fun thrown into my lessons, students will relish the nuances of words.

Evaluation

Individual or small-group conferences are the perfect place to reteach or reinforce the mini-lesson.

As I confer individually with the students and review their writing, I help those who are hesitant about using the thesaurus and cheer those on who have begun to use it.

As students continue to use the thesaurus, I notice an improvement in their writing and record this improvement in an anecdotal note.

At the end of writing workshop each day, we have about a five-minute whole-group sharing time, when students volunteer to share a sentence or paragraph they have written. If they have used a thesaurus, I encourage them to share the word they changed and why. This gives me another opportunity to evaluate how each student is using the thesaurus to improve his or her writing.

CHAPTER 10

How a Story Is Developed

OBJECTIVE Students will understand how a story is developed.

FICTION STORY MAPS

Story maps are visual aides that help students understand both the structure and meaning of a story.

To introduce my students to the elements of a story, I show them a simple four-square story map that shows the four basic elements of a story: *characters*, *setting*, *conflict* (problem), and *resolution* (solution). As students develop an understanding of these literary elements, we branch out, studying the story's events, theme, and point of view. I also introduce *round* and *flat* (major and minor) *characters* and *integral* and *backdrop settings.*

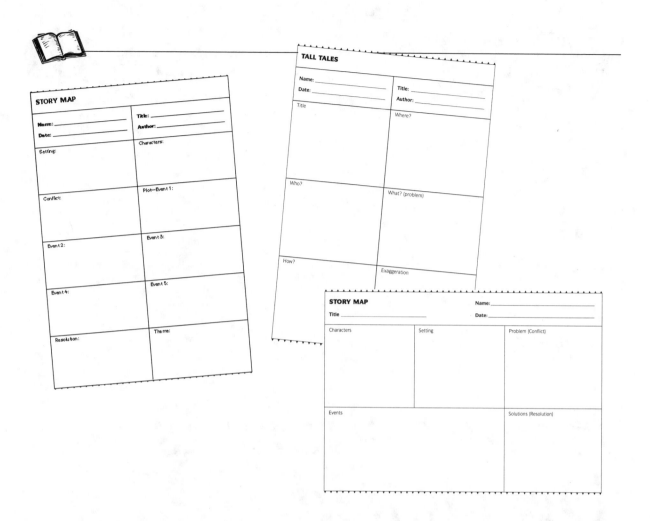

How I Do It

INTRODUCING THE ELEMENTS OF A STORY

For the first mini-lesson, I read aloud a short, interesting book. One of my favorites is a Caldecott Honor Book, *Mufaro's Beautiful Daughters* by John Steptoe (Scholastic, 1987). Since this is a picture book, I have students sit as close to me as possible so they can enjoy the illustrations.

Afterward, I ask students to name the characters in the story. I write the names on a graphic organizer that I have prepared ahead of time. This particular graphic organizer is a story map which has different sections for the elements of the story that we are studying. The characters are listed in the box labeled CHARACTERS. After discussing the setting of the story, I label another section SETTING and record what the students tell me about the setting.

The map has sections for CONFLICT and RESOLUTION (problem and solution), and we discuss and fill in these sections, too. For example, after our discussion of the book, Marina, a fourth grader,

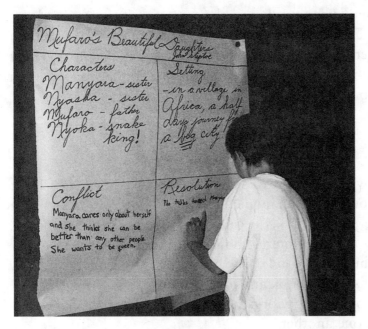

said, "The conflict is that Manyara cares only about herself and she thinks she can be better than any other people. She wants to be the queen." I wrote Marina's exact comment in the conflict box. Truthfully, I had thought that there was a different conflict, but Marina and her peers convinced me that she was correct. It is important to use the students' own words and not to try to get them to say something that they did not mean. All too often we try to put words in our students' mouths.

Pointing out how this conflict was resolved was not difficult for Marina's classmate, Kellen, who offered to write the resolution on the organizer himself: "The tables turned on Manyara and just the opposite happened. Nyasha became queen and Manyara became her servant." To help the students personalize the map, I frequently have them make colorful pictures to go in each section. My middle school students enjoy illustrating each section as much as the younger students do.

EXAMINING STORY EVENTS

In our next lesson, I talk with students about how John Steptoe resolved the problem of who should be the king's wife. This leads to a discussion of story events, and together we list the story's events in sequential order on the story map.

WHEN STORY MAPPING IS A NEW SKILL

I've found that if story mapping is a new exercise for students, they grasp it faster when I divide the lesson into two parts. So in the first lesson we concentrate on characters, setting, and conflict and resolution. In the second lesson we discuss the sequence of events that leads to the solution. The same story map may be used for both lessons—I simply fold under the Events section of the map so students don't get overwhelmed. In the second lesson, students unfold that section when they are ready to list the events sequentially.

PRACTICE IN PAIRS

Next, students work in pairs to make their own story maps. I ask them to choose one of the many picture books I have available in the classroom. I use picture books because they are shorter than novels and they usually are high-interest books. I never have enough of my own books for this activity so I check out many titles from the library. The student teams read a book and together make a story map. I leave time at the end of reading workshop for the students to share their story maps with one another.

CHARACTER STUDY

One of the most effective ways to dig deep in a story is to explore such questions as: How does an author develop a character? Do characters have to be real people? By reading different books, students discover that fictional characters can be just about anyone or anything. They can be animals that speak, such as Wilbur the pig and Charlotte the spider in E. B. White's *Charlotte's Web*, or objects that talk, such as the Tin Woodsman or Scarecrow in Frank L. Baum's *The Wonderful Wizard of Oz*. Every book I read aloud, as well as those children read in groups and independently, offers an opportunity to get at the heart of literature by studying character.

ROUND AND FLAT CHARACTERS

To help the students understand that not all characters have the same impact on a story but that all are essential, I introduce the concept of round and flat characters. One good way to approach this is to have students read aloud plays. This helps them see that there are big and small parts. Chris, for example, really objected that he did not have many lines to read. He was so disappointed that he refused to be in the play. Once I soothed his ego, I seized the opportunity to talk about round and flat characters.

To open the discussion, I put a small plate and a big round rubber ball on a table and ask students which one they notice first. Without

I discovered the terms round *and* flat *in Rebecca J. Luken's book,* A Critical Handbook of Children's Literature *(HarperCollins, 1990).*

fail, students notice the ball. I ask them why this is so. (It is larger than the plate and takes up more space.) From here I lead students into a discussion of flat and round characters. We discuss which characters in the play take up the most space and have the most lines. They are the round characters. The other characters are the flat characters. They take up little space or have few lines—but without them the play would not be complete.

Once again, I use John Steptoe's *Mufaro's Beautiful Daughters* to illustrate my lesson. "Which characters do you see as taking up the most space—which are the round characters?" I ask. "Manyara and Nyasha," students reply. Then I ask, "Why do they take up so much space in the story?"

This book works well because there are only two main characters; students don't have trouble identifying them. Next I ask them who the flat characters are in the book, or the characters that do not take up much space. The father, Mufaro, the king, the boy, and the old woman are all suggestions I hear. We analyze why they take up so little space and discover that they are mentioned only a few times and do very little talking; however, without them, the story would not be complete.

The students love the terms *flat* and *round*. As I read aloud, or when they are discussing books in literary circles, they enjoy pointing out the round and flat characters. When Jill, a sixth grader, was giving a book talk, she wrote the names of the round characters on a round balloon and listed the flat characters on a piece of wood. She used these as props for her book talk.

DYNAMIC AND STATIC CHARACTERS

Below and on page 102 are excerpts from responses written by fifth graders Amanda and Amy. We had been studying how authors used static and dynamic characters to tell their story, and as a follow-up to this lesson, the two girls wrote about the characters in their own book and stated why they thought they were either *static* or *dynamic*.

> The main character is a boy named Will who eventually becomes a dynamic character. The thing that interested me most was that Will changed in the same way that Hansi did in the book *Hansi*.

Amanda's response

101

> *Charlotte's Web* is a great book. The main character is
>
> Wilbur. Wilbur is a very wimp pig in the beginning but he
>
> turns out to be confident and brave towards the end.

Amy's response

Using familiar stories as models helps students quickly grasp the idea of dynamic and static characters. In Gary Paulsen's *Hatchet* we recall how helpless Brian was at the beginning of the story. During the story he goes through many changes as he learns to survive in the wilderness. When he comes out of the wilderness, he is independent and can solve his problems. He is a dynamic character. Another book that I use to illustrate this point is E. B. White's *Charlotte's Web*. Wilbur changes from a fun-loving little piglet to a pig who has feelings and is compassionate. Whereas Fern, the little girl who befriended Wilbur, did not change throughout the story. She's a static character. Usually the round (main) character in a book series such as *Nancy Drew*, *Cam Jansen*, or *The Sweet Valley Twins* is a static character. While these protagonists experience lots of excitement and interact with dynamic characters in each book, they themselves do not change.

SMALL-GROUP STUDIES

Students explore dynamic and static characters further in small groups, discussing and categorizing the characters they've come across in their class and independent reading. To record their ideas, I have them divide a piece of paper into two parts and label them *Dynamic* and *Static*. They write the characters' names and the book titles under the appropriate sections. If only one student has read a particular book, that's fine for her to add it to the chart. I move from group to group, listening to students and helping them as needed. I let students know when it is about five minutes from Share Time. Then we come together and go over our lists. I collect these lists as we will use them again in another mini-lesson.

The next day, students work in the same groups. I return their lists and ask them to decide which characters on their lists are round and which are flat. As a class, we then make some general observations.

◆ Flat characters are always static characters. The conflict of the story has no impact on them.

◆ Round characters can be both dynamic and static. Nancy Drew in the mystery series by the same name is a static character, but she is also a round character. Brian, in *Hatchet* is a round and a dynamic character.

BACKDROP AND INTEGRAL SETTINGS

Even very young children are aware of where a story takes place. *Goldilocks and the Three Bears* takes place in the bears' house. *The Three Billy Goats Gruff* takes place on a bridge. Children usually discover the setting on the very first page of the story, if not in the first paragraph. But as students' reading material becomes more complex, the setting is not always apparent on the first page. The author may take several chapters to establish his or her characters and their environment. Does this pose a problem for the readers? Yes. Students want the action to begin immediately and will often give up on a book that is "too slow." Here's how I encourage my students to stay with it.

Andrea was having difficulty getting involved in *The War with Grandfather* by Robert Kimmel Smith (Dell, 1984). After reading with her for a while, we discovered that the war was between the grandfather and his grandson, and it was over a bedroom. The author had written a paragraph describing in detail the grandson's bedroom. To help Andrea discover *why* the grandfather and the grandson were warring over this bedroom, I suggested that Andrea color a picture of the room according to the author's description. This exercise jump-started her interest in the book, and she flew through the rest of the story.

INTEGRAL SETTINGS

When my students give book talks or when I read a story aloud, I often ask such questions as: Could this story take place in another setting? Can this story be moved to another setting? What would happen if the author changed the setting? Children learn that some plots can be moved from one setting to another without significantly changing the story, but other stories could not survive if set in a different place.

In other words, if the setting is *integral*, the story really cannot take place anywhere other than where the author has placed it. The setting is essential to the plot. *Sarah Plain and Tall* by Patricia MacLachlan (HarperCollins, 1985) is an example of a story with an integral setting; the house and the prairies are essential to the story line.

BACKDROP SETTINGS

If the setting serves as a *backdrop*, the story could take place any-where without affecting the story line. Folktales often have backdrop settings: "Once upon a time in a far away country..." Because most children are familiar with Winnie the Pooh, I use A. A. Milne's *The House at Pooh Corner* as an example of a book with a backdrop set-ting. There is nothing distinctive about Pooh's house. It could be located in any forest.

As you and your students explore integral and backdrop settings, it's helpful to use a chart to record what you discover. I ask students to think about the books they are reading or have read and decide if the author intended the setting to be integral or backdrop. Our con-versation proceeds along these lines:

MRS. L: Think about the books you are reading or have read. Did the author make the setting integral or backdrop? After a suitable wait time, I say: Now that you have had a moment to think about your books, who would like to be the first one to share?

JILL: I am reading *The Diary of Anne Frank*. The setting is integral because the story would have to take place where the war is going on and where Anne and her family could hide.

MRS. L: Yes, I agree with you and I see others nodding their heads in agreement. Please write the title under the integral heading while we continue to share our ideas.

RACHEL: In September, I read *Ramona and Her Father*. That story could take place anywhere. So I guess the setting is backdrop.

We continue in this manner, sharing and discussing the different books we have read. We don't always agree but this is what stimulates the conversation.

Integral Setting	Backdrop Setting
Diary of Anne Frank	*Ramona and Her Father*
Hatchet	*Jessica's Secret*
Where the Red Fern Grows	*Tales of a Fourth Grade Nothing*
Sarah Plain and Tall	

WRITING ABOUT PLACE

New concepts become clearer to students when they explain them in their own words. So after we have completed group lessons on inte-gral and backdrop settings, I ask students to analyze the setting in the book they are reading, writing their analysis in their reading response journals. I also ask students to include a description of the setting. I encourage them to shut their eyes, make a mental picture of the setting, and then jot down images. This exercise makes it is easier for them to describe the setting in their own words.

Fifth grader Amy describes the setting of one of her favorite books:

> The setting of Charlottes Web is in a barn. The barn is smelly with the smells of manure piles and slops for the pigs to eat. The setting was influenced the plot because spiders are usually found hang around on barns because they find lots of dark corners for them to make their webs. Wilber met Charlotte at in the barn and that is when Charlotte helped him with his problems.

▲ ▲ ▲ ▲ ▲ ▲ ▲

Theme is the central idea of the story. Theme binds the narrative together. It is expressed through characters and events, but never in a dogmatic manner. In a well-written story, the theme is subtly woven into the narrative. When we finish reading the story, we feel we have learned something about people and life— we don't feel as though we've been lectured.

▼ ▼ ▼ ▼ ▼ ▼ ▼

THEME: THE AUTHOR'S MESSAGE

Theme can be a more elusive element of literature for students to grasp, but approaching it with the use of read-alouds really helps demystify it. For example, after reading *A Wrinkle in Time* as a class, I ask students if they think the author is trying to get across a message. Yes, Amy replied, and put the message in terms of good versus bad. One of her classmates said, "It isn't good—it is love." Paul elaborated on this by saying, "Love conquers evil." When reading Judy Blume's *The Tales of a Fourth Grade Nothing* (Dutton, 1972), my students decided the message was patience.

As I meet with literature or novel groups, we always discuss the message, or theme. Students need my guidance initially, but soon they can lead their own discussions. Here are two examples of students' insightfulness.

In her discussion of *Charlotte's Web*, Amy said, "The theme of *Charlottes's Web* is 'Being a good friend pays off.' That was the theme because Charlotte was a good friend to Wilbur and it paid off because Wilbur didn't die."

Daniel defined the message in *The Trumpet of the Swan* as "...never give up once you've set a goal."

When students feel comfortable identifying a theme in a story they're reading, I ask them to discuss it in their Reading Response Journals. After reading *The Door in the Wall*, Nicole wrote, "I think the theme of this book was that if you look hard enough there is always a door in the wall. Also to never give up and you will succeed." After reading *Treasure Island*, Amy wrote, "I think the theme of this story is 'Don't trust anyone anymore if they tell you lies or do bad things all the time.' I think that is the theme because Long John Silver kept tricking Jim Hawkins into believing he was a nice guy although he really killed people and went after the treasure like it was a race to win."

Follow-Up Activities _____

STORY MAPS FOR OTHER TYPES OF LITERATURE

Not all literature follows the same outline. Fantasy, fairy tales, folktales, and tall tales have small differences. When we study the different genres, my students and I work together analyzing the stories and determining the characteristics of each. Using these characteristics we develop story maps for the different types of literature.

USING THE ELEMENTS OF STORIES IN WRITING

We use the same story maps that students complete when they read a story to help them plan stories of their own. For instance, when I

want students to write their own folktales I begin by spending several days reading folktales and discussing the characteristics of this genre. Together we develop and complete a folktale story map.

I then model how this folktale story map can be used to help them write their own folktales. I make a transparency of a folktale story map. I model how I develop my own original story, talking about the story as I develop it. It is important that students understand exactly what you want them to do.

Next, I have students use the folktale story map to help them organize their ideas for their own story. They then get together with a buddy and tell the story using the ideas on their map. They offer each other suggestions and refine their story maps before they begin writing. This prewriting step is very effective, and usually results in more focused—and accomplished—stories.

After organizing her ideas on a story map, Emily wrote a delightful story called "Whiskers."

STORY MAP

Name: Emily	Title: Whiskers
Date: April 13, 94	Author: Emily Fischer
Setting: Country	Characters: Mrs. Daple Mr. Daple, and the cat
Conflict: Loved cat very much but needed money.	Plot—Event 1: Found out about Cat's whiskers.
Event 2: Pulled them and out of the cat's mouth came $100 bill.	Event 3: Became very rich. But then cat died. Went back to little house.
Event 4: Visited the cats grave and then one day cat came back to life.	Event 5: People never pulled cats whiskers again and the cat lived forever.
Resolution: New how much they loved the cat and didn't pull cat's whiskers.	Theme: Money isn't better then love, don't let money take control of your life.

Draft 1
April 15, 94
Emily

Whiskers

Page 1
Mr. and Mrs. Daple stared at the cat. (their eyes as big as saucers) The cat was as black as sut. What happend to Mr. and Mrs. Daple could never have happend to anyone else, or so they thought. Something happened. Something lucky and something fearful. The cat's whiskers shined like stars in the sky. they were different, special. They were magic. Mrs. Daple reached down and pulled the whiskers. Halting, the cat descended its mouth and spit out a $100 bill.

Evaluation

TEACHER OBSERVATION

After students complete their story maps, I review them, which helps me see whether each student has comprehended the meaning of the story. Sometimes I ask students to mark which characters are round and flat and to indicate whether the setting is integral or backdrop.

BOOK TALKS

Book talks are an excellent method to evaluate each student. Through his discussion of the book, I can determine whether or not the student understands the concept of conflict and resolution, as well as other elements of the story.

STORY WRITING

As I read students' stories, I note whether they have well-drawn characters, well-defined settings, conflict, and events that lead up to resolutions. As I see the need for additional help, I reteach to an individual or a small group of students.

AUDIO- OR VIDEOTAPE ASSESSMENT

An audiotaping or videotaping of a book talk helps both me and my students evaluate their learning. Students can review the tapes on their own, or in conference with me.

CHAPTER 11

Point of View

OBJECTIVE

Students will understand that the point of view presented is determined by the author. Students will understand that different points of view exist in different books. Students will understand that people have different points of view about a topic.

WE ALL SEE THINGS DIFFERENTLY

When I introduce the concept of point of view, I personalize it by relating it to an experience students are very familiar with—eating lunch in the school cafeteria! I ask students to pretend that someone has complained that the cafeteria is too noisy. Working in groups of three or four, students are to role play how different people might view the cafeteria and its noise. I write the names of various people involved with the cafeteria on pieces of paper—the principal, the cafeteria hostess, the students, the custodian, the teacher, and visiting parents. I give each group a name and ask them to develop a skit that shows their person's reaction to the complaint that the cafeteria is too noisy. The students love to role play so they really put a lot of energy into their skits. After the skits have been performed, the students and I discuss how people have different views about the same situation. I have discovered that this is a wonderful way to lead the students into a discussion of point of view in literature.

How I Do It

To introduce point of view in literature, I read aloud a short familiar version of *The Three Little Pigs*. Then I read *The True Story of the Three Little Pigs* by Jon Scieszka (Viking, 1989). After enjoying both tales, we compare and contrast them. The Venn diagram shown here will give you an idea of how we go about our discussion.

I make certain that the students understand that in *The True Story of the Three Little Pigs,* the tale is told from the wolf's point of view, while in the classic version the author tells the story. I encourage students to think about and discuss how point of view changes the story for the reader.

Next, I read aloud *Rip Van Winkle, A Classic Tale* by Washington Irving, retold by Dr. Alvin Granowsky (Steck-Vaughn, 1993) and then Granowsky's *Wake Up, Rip Van Winkle*, which appears in the same book.

As was true in *The Three Little Pigs*, the classic version is told from the point of view of the author, while in the updated rendition, a character—Rip's daughter—tells the story. (According to Rip's daughter, Rip did not sleep for 20 years!)

After we've savored both stories, I divide the class into groups of two or three and have them complete a Venn diagram comparing the stories. Students add colorful illustrations to the diagrams.

VENN DIAGRAM

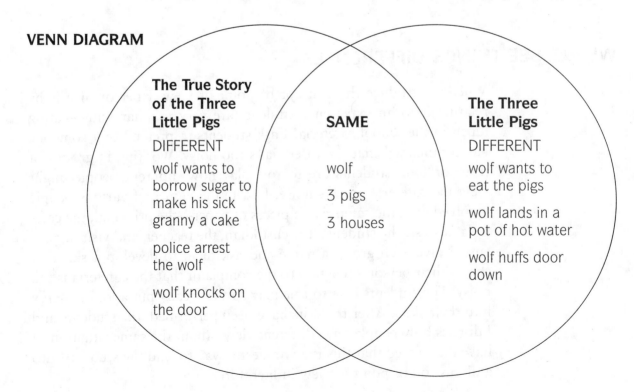

The True Story of the Three Little Pigs

DIFFERENT

wolf wants to borrow sugar to make his sick granny a cake

police arrest the wolf

wolf knocks on the door

SAME

wolf

3 pigs

3 houses

The Three Little Pigs

DIFFERENT

wolf wants to eat the pigs

wolf lands in a pot of hot water

wolf huffs door down

Sept. 25

Dear Mrs. Loose,

In the fairy tale, Jack and the Beanstalk the author is telling the story through Jack. We all felt sorry for for Jack. If the author told the story through the giant we would have found out that the giant had lots of things stolen from him. That is why he is mad.

Your student
John

A Reading Journal entry

▲ ▲ ▲ ▲ ▲ ▲ ▲

First-person point of view is when the writer chooses a character to tell the story. In a first-person story, the reader lives, acts, feels, and thinks as the person telling the story.

▼ ▼ ▼ ▼ ▼ ▼ ▼

FIRST-PERSON POINT OF VIEW

Using the same books I mentioned above, I make transparencies of pages from each book that convey the point of view, so students can see it for themselves. Students see the use of the word *I* on a page of *The True Story of the Three Little Pigs* and know that the wolf is telling the story. Likewise, they can study pages from *Wake Up, Rip Van Winkle* and see that the narrator is Rip's daughter, not the author or another narrator.

I articulate for children that the wolf and the daughter relate what the other characters in the story say, but they never express the other character's feelings or opinions since they do not know them. *They are only telling it as they understand it.*

To reinforce this concept, I engage students in a discussion of another story they all know and love, *Pigs Might Fly* by Dick King-Smith (Scholastic, 1980). We note how the pigs all talk about the Pigman, and that they are not very complementary about him. I ask students to share what they think the Pigman would say about himself if *he* were telling the story.

Reading the four stories and introducing the concept of point of view in literature take several lessons over a period of several days. During this period of time I have many traditional fairy tale and folktale books in the room, as well as some of the more modern transformed fairy tale books. *The True Story of the Three Little Pigs* is a tranformed fairy tale. Other transformed fairy tales that my students enjoy are the following:

Jim and the Beanstalk by R. Briggs (Puffin Books, 1973)
The Principal's New Clothes by S. Calmenson (Scholastic, 1989)
Prince Cinders by B. Cole (Colins, 1989)
Ruby by M. Emberly (Little Brown, 1990)
Pondlarker by F. Gwynne (Simon & Schuster, 1990)
Pizza for Breakfast by M. Kovalski (Morrow, 1990)
The Paper Bag Princess by R. Munsch (Annick Press, 1980)
Somebody and the Three Blairs by M. Tolhurst (Orchard, 1990)
Ugh by A. Yorinks (Farrar, Straus, & Giroux, 1990)

I have my students read the books together, often in pairs. One student can retell the original story while the other tries her hand at retelling the story from another character's point of view.

A Reading Journal activity I find effective is to have students select a fairy tale, identify who is telling the story, and discuss how it would change if someone else were telling it.

THIRD-PERSON POINT OF VIEW

We continue to examine *The Three Little Pigs* and *Rip Van Winkle*. I ask students: Who is telling these stories? I guide students to realize that in *The Three Little Pigs* the narrator is telling the story, but the point of view is that of the pigs. After all, the wolf is made out to be the villain while the little pigs are innocent victims. Jon Scieszka tells the story from the point of view of the wolf; that is why it is fun to read.

Now we turn our attention to the classic tale of Rip Van Winkle. To prepare for the lesson, I select a page that shows that this version of the story is written in an omniscient point of view. I make a transparency of the page, checking to see that the print is large enough for students to read and that there is enough space between the lines so that students can mark with colored projector pens. Here is the page I use:

A simple, good-natured fellow named Rip Van Winkle lived in the village. He was descended from the Van Winkles who had battled bravely at Stuyvesant's side in the quest for territory. Rip, however, had inherited little of his ancestors' nature. Rip was simply a carefree man, always ready with a smile and a story. People throughout the village knew Rip as a kind neighbor and a friendly chap.

Sadly, Rip Van Winkle led the life of a hen-pecked husband. His wife found fault with everything he did. The quarrels between him and his wife raged from early in the morning until late in the evening. From Dame Van Winkle, Rip learned the virtues of patience and suffering.

While his own wife found only fault with Rip, the other wives of the village found much to appreciate in him. The village women always took Rip's part in his family's squabbles and laid all the blame on Dame Van Winkle.

The children of the village adored Rip because he made playthings for them, flew kites with them and told them long stories about ghosts. Wherever Rip went, children crowded around him. The little ones hung on the man's coat, clamored for his attention, and played countless tricks on Rip. Dogs never barked when this good-hearted man came into their neighborhood.

Rip Van Winkle
written by Washington Irving
retold by Dr. Alvin Granowsky
(Steck-Vaughn, 1993)

After students have read the passage aloud or to themselves, we go through it, paragraph by paragraph. I reread the first paragraph and then think out loud so students can hear how I determine the point of view.

Rip is from a famous family. He lives in a village. He is simple, good-natured, kind, carefree, and friendly. He enjoys telling stories. The author certainly does know a lot about Rip.

Then I ask the students to read the second paragraph to themselves and share their thoughts. As we think through the paragraphs we discover that there is more about Rip in the subsequent paragraphs, as well as information about his wife, the other wives in the village, the children, and even the dogs. Sometimes I make a chart with headings: Rip, Wife, Other Women, Children, Dogs. Under each heading I list the characteristics of each.

CHARACTERISTICS

Rip	wife	other women	children	dog
simple	nagged	liked Rip	adored Rip	liked Rip
good-natured	quarrelsome			playful

It doesn't take students long to discover that Rip himself is not telling the story. It is the author who knows about every person in the story—what they think, how they act, and how they feel. I tell students: We know it's the author's point of view, but is there a character the author kind of favors? I guide students to see that the author tells the story in such a way that we see the story through Rip's eyes. We feel sorry for him.

At this time I explain the terms *third-person point of view* and *omniscient point of view*. Since the story favors Rip, the point of view is third person. Because the author is the narrator and knows everything about the character, it is also told from *omniscient* point of view.

To reinforce this concept I ask students to write entries in their reading journals reflecting on the fairy tales and folktales they have been reading. I ask them to identify one that is written with a third-person point of view. I invite them to discuss which character's point of view is being presented and what would happen if another character's view was expressed. Since students have been reading fairy tales and folktales for a few days at this point, they have a background of stories from which to choose.

Follow-Up Activities

CHARTS

To keep the concept of point of view in literature fresh in children's minds I post two pieces of tag board on the wall. I label one "First Person Point of View" and the other "Omniscient Point of View." As students read books, I encourage them to write the titles of the books on the appropriate charts. I suggest that they confer with a peer who has also read the book.

COMIC STRIPS

I have children locate a comic strip that they want to rewrite from a different point of view.

PERSUASIVE PARAGRAPHS

A study of point of view combines beautifully with exercises on writing persuasive paragraphs. I take ideas from Chapter 6 on writing paragraphs and show students how to apply these concepts to writing a persuasive paragraph. Before children begin writing, I tell them that, in the course of their paragraphs, they have to develop their viewpoint and support that view with facts. Their work with point of view significantly enhances their ability to do this.

You have probably heard the story of the moss-covered rock but that does not make it true. So before I become the big bad spider here, I'm going to make this wrong a right! So sit down, relax and enjoy the true story of the moss-covered rock Oh, by the way my name is Anasi, the misunderstood spider...

Alison's newfangled folktale

LETTERS

In a similar exercise, I invite students to share their point of view through letter writing. I allow students to write all sorts of letters—from writing their Congresspeople to state their opinion on a topic such as gun control, to penning a note to their parents explaining their point of view about something. One group of students I taught wanted a longer play time at lunch so they wrote letters to the principal. They were so convincing, the principal came to class to discuss *his* point of view!

NEWFANGLED FAIRY TALES

After analyzing the format of a fairy tale or folk-

Loyalist: Why do you want to be independent from Britain? We're British, we're part of Britain we should be proud.
Patriot: I want to be independent from Britain because Britain is a strong country and I don't want to be part of them anymore.
Loyalist: But why?
Patriot: I want to be a new country with new rules such as you have to be 21 to be in the House of Burgesses, or only the members could choose who could join the House of Burgesses. I won't new things to happen like people that don't have any money will get some each month. New adventures like finding some mysterious caves. I want to start a whole different point of view. Why do you want to be a loyalist?
Loyalist: Because I think we should stick with the country we were from in the first place. I'm proud to be British.
    Patriot and Loyalist leave.

Viewpoints of loyalists and patriots

tale, I have students rewrite a favorite one from a different character's point of view. I have found that my students enjoy this activity so we usually take these stories through the complete writing process. We then share our stories with students in a primary classroom.

SOCIAL STUDIES CONNECTIONS

There are always at least two sides to every story. During our study of Colonial America, I have students show me that they understand the different viewpoints of the loyalists and the patriots. Jamie and Hilary wrote this dialogue (left) between a loyalist and a patriot.

When studying the Civil War and slavery in America, I ask my students to write a paragraph as a slave might view a certain situation and another paragraph conveying the slave owner's take on the same event. Or students can write letters about an event from the point of view of a slave girl, as well as from the viewpoint of the slave owner's daughter. The students learn a lot from these writing experiences—and I learn a great deal about my students.

Evaluation

TEACHER EVALUATION

As I read students' Reading Journal entries and listen to them discussing point of view in various books, I note the depth of their understanding. I make anecdotal notes on the strengths and needs of each student so I can plan future lessons based on these needs.

I can also evaluate students' understanding of the content areas by listening to oral presentations and reading the students' writing to see if the students understand the different views of the loyalists and patriots, slaves and their owners, and so on.

115

STUDENT AND TEACHER EVALUATION

After the students have rewritten a fairy tale from another point of view, they confer with a friend and revise it together. They assess the needs and make any necessary revisions. Then I confer with the author and together we double check that the point of view is consistent throughout the story. It is important that assessment and evaluation are ongoing. Revising and editing are part of the writing process, but they are also important components of assessment and evaluation.

CHAPTER 12

Writing Dialogue

OBJECTIVE   Students will write effective dialogue.

▲ ▲ ▲ ▲ ▲ ▲

A speaker tag is a phrase that identifies the person who is talking. John said, Ted cried loudly, *and* answered Jane *are some examples.*

▼ ▼ ▼ ▼ ▼ ▼

I developed this mini-lesson when my students were happily cranking out fiction with an enthusiasm that outpaced their knowledge of the mechanics of writing conversation. All of us were frustrated with the results. At the time, I was reading aloud *Shiloh* by Phyllis Reynolds Naylor (Dell, 1991), and my students loved it. It didn't take me long to realize that I had the perfect vehicle for teaching students the rules of writing dialogue.

Shiloh has wonderful examples of conversation. Since then I have found many other examples of dialogue that can also be used. I am forever on the lookout for pages of conversation that show the speaker tags in different places in sentences. I feel like I've found a gold mine when I find periods, question marks, commas, and exclamation points in a dialogue all on the same page. I immediately make a copy of the page so I can use it in future lessons. I have discovered pages that contain good examples of dialogue in our basals, in the books I am reading aloud to the class, and in books the students are reading. The lessons are most successful, however, when the students are familiar with the text.

How I Do It

This page I chose from *Shiloh* is a wonderful example as it shows how commas, periods, question marks, and exclamation points are used in conversation. It also shows the speaker tags in the middle of a statement, as well as at the end. To save time when making the transparency, I always try enlarging the text on a copy machine. If I can't get it large enough, I type my own copy—it is essential that all the students be able to read the text when it is projected on the screen.

I stop. *"I'm lookin' to find me a snake stick,"* I say as if to myself.

"I'm looking to find me a snake stick," Dara Lynn says.

I don't pay her no mind at all. Just start walkin' along the edge of the yard, picking up a stick here, a stick there, Dara Lynn tagging along behind.

"It's got to have the longest handle and a good strong fork on the end," I say, *"because that was the biggest, meanest snake I ever saw in my life."*

Dara Lynn stops dead still. She couldn't say all that right if she tried, but she's not interested anymore in trying. *"What snake?"* she says.

"Snake I saw up on the hill this mornin'," I tell her. *"Must have been four, five feet long, just lookin' for somebody's leg to wrap itself around."*

Dara Lynn don't go a step farther. Becky don't even come down off the porch.

"What you going to do when you find it?" Dara Lynn asks.

"Try to keep it from bitin' me, first. Pick it up with my stick, second, put it in a sack, and carry it clear on up past the Shiloh schoolhouse, let it out in the woods there. Won't kill it unless I have to."

"Kill it!" says Dara Lynn. *"Git your gun and blow its head off."*

"You been watchin' too much stuff on TV, Dara Lynn," I tell her. *"Even snakes got the right to live."*

Shiloh by Phyllis Reynolds Naylor
(Dell, 1991)

SETTING THE STAGE

I project the transparency onto the screen and ask a student to read the passage out loud. Since it is familiar text, most students should be able to read it. I then state my objective—to discover the rules that a writer follows when writing dialogue. I write our objective on top of a chart the students will work with later in the lesson.

WHO SAID IT?

Next I ask the students to identify the different speakers in the conversation. Since there are two speakers in this conversation, I ask two students to come to the overhead and circle the speaker tags, using a different color marker for each speaker. I then ask for other volunteers to come and draw a line under the dialogue using the same color marker as the speaker tag. The different colors enable the students to see the format the author uses to write conversation.

After the speaker tags have been circled and the dialogue underlined, we begin our search for the rules for writing conversation. I lead the search by having students find answers to these questions:

I stop. _"I'm lookin' to find me a snake stick,"_ (I say) as if to myself.

"I'm looking to find me a snake stick," (Dara Lynn says.)

I don't pay her no mind at all. Just start walkin' along the edge of the yard, picking up a stick here, a stick there, Dara Lynn tagging along behind.

"It's got to have the longest handle and a good strong fork on the end," (I say,) _"because that was the biggest, meanest snake I ever saw in my life."_

Dara Lynn stops dead still. She couldn't say all that right if she tried, but she's not interested anymore in trying. _"What snake?"_ (she says.)

"Snake I saw up on the hill this mornin'," (I tell her.) _"Must have been four, five feet long, just lookin' for somebody's leg to wrap itself around."_

Dara Lynn don't go a step farther. Becky don't even come down off the porch. _"What you going to do when you find it?"_ (Dara Lynn asks.)

"Try to keep it from bitin' me, first. Pick it up with my stick, second, put it in a sack, and carry it clear on up past the Shiloh schoolhouse, let it out in the woods there. Won't kill it unless I have to."

"Kill it!" (says Dara Lynn.) _"Git your gun and blow its head off."_

"You been watchin' too much stuff on TV, Dara Lynn," (I tell her.) _"Even snakes got the right to live."_

◆ What marks do you see around the words the speaker says?

◆ Let's look at the periods. Do they stand alone or are they used with other punctuation marks? Do you see any pattern?

◆ Where do you find commas in this dialogue? Is there a pattern?

By this time, students should be searching for a pattern for the question marks and exclamation points. If they are not, I continue my questioning.

After students discover the patterns, I encourage them to restate each pattern as a rule for writing dialogue. On the chart paper where I listed the objective, I write the heading "Rules for Writing Conversation" and then record the rules students suggest, careful to write them exactly as students expressed them.

As much as I am tempted to dictate the rules to students, I have discovered that they remember them better when they discover the rules themselves.

Rules for Writing Dialogue

◆ Put quotation marks around the speaker's exact words.

◆ Capitalize the first word the speaker says.

◆ If the dialogue is first, a comma, a question mark, or an exclamation point comes after it.

◆ The comma, question mark, period, and exclamation marks come inside the quotation marks.

◆ When the dialogue is first and the speaker tag is last, the dialogue is followed by a comma and not by a period, unless it is a question or an exclamation.

◆ When the speaker tag is last in the sentence, it is followed by a period.

◆ Change paragraphs when you change speakers.

Rules have more meaning to students when written exactly as students say them.

I keep this chart where students can see it for reference when they are writing dialogue. They soon discover that there are other rules to add to the chart, such as:

When the speaker tag is first, it is separated from the quotation by a comma.

PRACTICE MAKES PERFECT

To give students additional practice, I take another page from *Shiloh*. I like to use samples from the same text, but there is nothing wrong with choosing a sample from another book. This time, however, I

120

leave out all of the punctuation before handing it out as a worksheet to students.

MANAGEMENT HINT: *When copying text for the students to replace the punctuation, I leave out only the punctuation that relates to the dialogue.*

> *I wait until everyone is out of the kitchen and sitting around on the back porch to catch the breeze. As usual Becky and Dara Lynn whoop and tumble around in the grass, glad for an audience, and after I sit a respectable amount of time, I say Think I'll take my .22 and go up the far hill awhile*
>
> *What you figure on shooting this time of evening Dad asks*
> *Just workin' on my aim I tell him See how good I can hit when the light's dim*
> *Don't you ever, never, aim your gun toward this house or yard Ma says*
>
> *Shiloh* by Phyllis Reynolds Naylor
> (Dell, 1991)

I have students work in pairs to replace the missing punctuation marks. I encourage students to refer to the rules on their chart. When most of the groups are finished, I place a transparency of that worksheet on the overhead projector. I invite different students to come forward and put in the punctuation marks. I encourage students to add punctuation marks that they may have missed and correct any mistakes on their own papers. I also encourage them to challenge the class if they think a different punctuation mark should have been used. They soon discover that the meaning of a sentence can change if they use different punctuation than the author used.

To provide students with additional practice in editing dialogue, I make a transparency of a piece of writing which contains errors. The piece is one that I or a former student have written. We edit the piece together. Before I begin editing, however, I always read it aloud or ask one of the students to read it. Familiarizing students with the text makes it easier for them to edit it.

HE SAID, SHE SAID

As I read students' work, I often notice that they use *said* over and over in their speaker tags. To help them vary this speaker tag, we look at samples of dialogue in our trade books and list all the different words used instead of *said*. Again, a chart is a splendid way to display these words so that students can refer to it when they are writing. Students can also refer to the thesaurus for still more options. Sometimes

I feel I have too many charts in my room, so I have students keep their own individual lists in their writing folders.

> Said
>
> | | |
> |---|---|
> | cried | shouted |
> | asked | roared |
> | called | answered |
> | uttered | thought |
> | remarked | replied |
> | protested | repeated |
> | whispered | |

SAY IT WITH FEELING

"Mrs. Laase, this author uses lots of words in her speaker tags. Which one should I choose?"

While looking for variations on the word *said,* students discovered that a speaker tag frequently contains adverbs and prepositional phrases that describe the verb. To help all students understand this, I send them on a scavenger hunt through their books. They read for ten minutes. When they find a descriptive speaker tag that they like, they mark it with a strip of paper and continue reading. At the end of ten minutes, they share some of their favorite descriptive speaker tags. There was a noticeable change in the way they used speaker tags after this discovery.

ordered in a stern voice   asked anxiously

NO SPEAKER TAG?

As students look for descriptive speaker tags, they may discover that sometimes there is no speaker tag at all. Through discussion, I lead them to verbalize why a speaker tag is not always necessary. If it is a new paragraph it has to be a different speaker, and the context of the conversation makes it clear who is talking.

EDITING STRATEGY

After a student edits his own piece, he meets with a partner. Together they read one of their writings. They look at the dialogue rules on the chart and, jointly, they apply the rules to the piece. I also encourage each of them to take on a role of a speaker in the story and read it as a play. This is an easy way to see if a new paragraph begins whenever the speaker changes.

Follow-Up Activities

COMIC STRIPS

I use comic strips for a wide variety of activities with my students. The speech bubbles help students to see and understand the use of conversation and quotation marks. When I find a comic my students will enjoy, I block out the dialogue using liquid paper and make a copy of it for each student or group of students. They use the picture clues and their imaginations to write new dialogue. These are fun to post in the room so that students can see how others interpreted the pictures.

Sometimes I have students cut out a favorite comic and bring it to class. I assign them the task of rewriting it as dialogue and to embellish it to make it a story. The students need to know the rules for writing conversation to do this successfully!

My students also create comic strips based on books they are reading. I suggest they study the layout of various comics and then try their hand at writing one. This is how Emily turned an event in *Catwings* by Ursula K. LeGuin (Scholastic, 1988) into a comic strip.

FANTASY, FAIRY TALES, TALL TALES

The lessons on writing dialogue can also be introduced when students write a specific type of fiction such as fantasy, fairy tales, or tall tales.

Personally, I like to expose the students to the rules for writing dialogue before we get into fantasy writing. Fantasy, tall tales, and fairy tales need dialogue and require a different writing style than ordinary fiction. I know my students find it easier to learn to write these types of stories when they only have to concentrate on the new writing style rather than on the new writing style plus the rules for writing conversation.

The Little Red Hood

by Michael

Click! "This is Dan Rather on Channel 4 News with Mr. Wolf. This is his story."

"Hi. Everybody thinks they know what happened that dreaded day when I was convicted of that little brat's crime. I'm the supposedly mean old wolf who was framed for that small pip squeak's crime against her dear old granny -- just because I'm a wolf and I was there. I am a very nice and tame wolf unlike my vicious ancestors. Of course we wolves have to eat, but I had **no** intention of eating her! You see this is how it really happened . . ."

USING DIALOGUE IN THE CONTENT AREAS

In the content areas, students can share their reports through comic strips and plays. This is another way to integrate language arts skills across the curriculum.

PLAYS

During our study of famous women, the students are encouraged to be creative in the way they share their information on the women they research. Julia chose to write a play about Elizabeth Blackwell.

Julia had read several plays so she was familiar with the format. She knew a play contained dialogue, but that it is written differently than the conversation in a story. After looking at a few plays and using them as models, Julia wrote this delightful short script about Elizabeth Blackwell.

Elizabeth Blackwell

Narrator: On February 2, 1821, Elizabeth Blackwell was born. When she was old enough she didn't study embroidery, music, and art – subjects usual youg ladies studied.

Aunt Barbara: Anna and Marianne, my little girls, always do as they are told, but that Elizabeth is a very difficult child. It's too bad she was born a girl. she is strong-willed, and independent like a boy. She's going to cause a lot of trouble some day.

Narrator: And cause trouble she did!

Elizabeth: My father encouraged me to study math, Greek, Latin, and history. After studying I dreamed about many jobs and decided to be a doctor.

Narrator: They moved to America in 1832. She received a better education in America than would have been possible in England. During that time many famous people visited her house to wish her luck.

Actress: I'm very, very glad that people have started to notice women's rights.

Narrator: She attended a small school of medicine in Geneva, New York.

Elizabeth: It's not fair. I have completed many years of medical school, gotten the best grades in my class, and cannot study further because I'm a woman.

Narrator: Elizabeth went to Paris, France to observe doctors in a maternity home. On her first night there, Elizabeth helped a midwife deliver eight babies. Then she went to England and met Florence Nightingale.

Elizabeth: England is great, Florence. I can't believe I'm leaving it again, but I want to talk about improving living conditions for everyone, especially the poor.

Narrator: She returned to New York in 1851 and saw poor people and sick people living unhealthy lives. She began writing and speaking about the importance of healthy habits.

Elizabeth: I'm opening a clinic for the poor to teach prople the importance of preventing sickness as well as curing sickness.

Narrator: She founded the New York Infirmary and Training School so that other women could train to be doctors. This was Elizabeth Blackwell's life, the first woman doctor of the modern times.

Evaluation

ANECDOTAL NOTES

As students learn how to write dialogue using the correct punctuation, I keep anecdotal notes on their individual progress. As I see a need for additional help, I zero in on that student or group of students and reteach the concept that is causing difficulty.

CONFERENCES

Through student/teacher conferences, I have the opportunity to examine students' work in detail. I praise a job well done and give additional help as needed. When I confer with students, I have them read their dialogue aloud. Reading aloud helps them hear when there is a change in speakers.

DIALOGUE MASTERY CHECKLIST

A Dialogue Mastery Checklist can be kept for each student (see example on page 127). As each student's work that contains dialogue is read, the skills used—and not used—can be recorded on the checklist. This can help group students according to their needs for reteaching. This checklist can be used in conjunction with the overall Writing Mechanics Checklist, on which mastery of other types of punctuation is noted.

PEER CONFERENCES

When students confer with each other, they are evaluating their work. Together, they use the rules for writing dialogue to make the necessary corrections on their papers. By listening in on their conversations, I can gain insight into their understanding.

STUDENT SELF-EVALUATION

I encourage students to self-evaluate their work and set goals for improvement. The students use the Dialogue Mastery Checklist to aid them in editing and evaluating their work.

DIALOGUE MASTERY CHECKLIST

Name:_____

Skill:_____   **Mastery Date:** _____

Capitalizes first word of speaker_____

Varies speaker tags

    Beginning of sentences _____

    Middle of sentences _____

    End of sentences _____

    Synonyms for *said*_____

    Descriptive words with verb _____

    No speaker tag_____

Uses punctuation marks correctly

    Periods _____

    Commas _____

    Question marks _____

    Exclamation points _____

    Quotation marks _____

    Changes paragraphs for each speaker _____

_____

_____

_____

_____

_____

_____

_____

CHAPTER 13

Writing Lead Sentences

OBJECTIVE
Students will write lead sentences that catch the reader's attention.

Nasha couldn't wait to get older. She was sick of being told that she was too young to go hunting.

When Adrianna brought her story about Nasha the lion to a revision conference, I was thrilled when I read her lead sentences. This was evidence that she had understood the lessons that we had had on writing interesting lead sentences and was now applying the skills learned to her own writing. Her first draft of this story began like this: *There once lived a lion family in a jungle in Africa. There lived a mama lion, a daddy lion, and a baby lion named Nasha.* As Adrianna worked on her story, she went back and revised the beginning sentences until she felt she had a powerful opening.

How I Do It

"**O**nce upon a time…" may be a tried-and-true way to start a story, but I want to expose my students to other ways to catch the readers' attention. The first thing I do is search through literature books for good examples of dynamic lead sentences. When I find a book with a great lead sentence, I file away that information so when I am ready to present this lesson I can pull out those books. Normally I like to use literature the students are familiar with, but for this lesson that is not a requirement. In fact, it helps if the students don't know the story—they can better hear how the lead sentences catch the readers' attention.

SAMPLES OF GREAT LEAD SENTENCES IN FICTION

Lois Lowry opens her book *Anastasia, Ask your Analyst* (Dell, 1984) with this descriptive paragraph:

> *"Mom!" shouted Anastasia as she clattered up the back steps and into the kitchen after school. "Guess what Meredith Halberg gave me! Just what I've been wanting! And it didn't cost anything!"*

Another opener I like to use comes from *Downriver* by Will Hobbs (Bantam, 1991):

> *I stumbled on a rock that was barely sticking up, my legs were that tired. Flailing for balance, with the pack working against me, I slipped in the mud and almost went down. I still couldn't believe this was really happening. I couldn't believe my dad had done this to me.*

I continue with more samples from fiction books.

> *I shall never forget the first time I laid these now tired old eyes on our visitor. I had been left home by the family with the admonition to take care of the house until they returned. That's something they always say to me when they go out: "Take care of the house, Harold. You're the watchdog."* (*Bunnicula* by James Howe; Avon, 1979)

> *Walking back to camp through the swamp, Sam wondered whether to tell his father what he had seen.* (*The Trumpet of the Swan* by E. B. White; HarperCollins, 1970)

Together, my students and I have a wonderful time reading aloud the lead sentences and discussing why we think they are riveting. I ask students: What did the author do to catch our attention, and what do we think the story will be about based on the title and the lead sentences? After I have hooked my students' interest, I send them back to the books they are reading to sleuth out good lead sentences. They also are free to share lead sentences that are not good.

I do have one rule, however. Students must always defend their opinions. For example, Jasmine backed up her rave review of the first page of *The Secret of the Indian* by Lynne Reid Banks (Avon, 1990) by telling us that phrases like "there was a lengthy pause," "her face drained of color," and "she could hardly speak" made her realize that this would be an exciting book.

In addition to using the books students happen to be reading, I pass out three or four fiction books to each student. I ask them to read the lead sentences in these books and then share with the class those they think are effective. A happy chaos usually ensues, as children scramble to claim books—the lead sentences did what they are supposed to do!

STUDENTS WRITE LEAD SENTENCES

Since the objective of this lesson is to have students write great lead sentences I now have them take out a story they have written or one on which they're currently working. I encourage them to rework the beginning sentences. How can they make them even stronger? Everyone who is willing is encouraged to share. Marina liked the way she had revised the beginning of her story. Her original draft went like this:

> I go to Monument Top School in Glade Park. I don't get very good grades, but we don't care. Oh yeah, I forgot to tell you about my club.

She eagerly read the second draft of the beginning of her story:

> Guess what? We just got a new club member. She moved to Glade Park on the Monument. Her name is Sophie Wilkeor. She is very interesting as she knows a lot about Anasasi Indians and petroglyphs. She wants to learn about rocks so Jennifer and I asked her to join our club.

Hearing examples of strong lead sentences that their classmates have written is a powerful motivator for the other students. Now with the experience of recognizing great lead sentences in their own stories and listening to their peers read their revised lead sentences, my students now have the background knowledge to write lead sentences that catch the reader's attention.

LEAD SENTENCES IN NONFICTION

I often ask my students to respond to what they have learned in science, math, and social studies. To illustrate that there are more interesting ways to begin a response than by saying, "I learned that…" I

model good lead sentences in writing nonfiction in the same way that I modeled writing them in fiction. I begin by searching through non-fiction literature until I find lead sentences that will make exciting examples. Jean Fritz's books are my favorites to use.

Jean Fritz opens her book *Bully for You, Teddy Roosevelt!* (Scholastic, 1991) with these arresting, delightful sentences:

> *What did Theodore Roosevelt want to do? Everything. And all at once if possible. Plunging head-long into life, he refused to waste a single minute. Among other things, he studied birds, shot lions, roped steer, fought a war, wrote books, and discovered the source of a mystery river in South America.*

I also like to use her books about Ben Franklin and Paul Revere for samples of good lead sentences.

> *In 1706 Boston was so new that its streets were still being named. For 5 years the town officials had been thinking up names and they hadn't finished yet. So far they had Cow Lane, Flounder Lane, Turn Again Alley, Half-Square Court, Pond Street, Sliding Alley, Milk Street, and many others.*
> *(What's the Big Idea, Ben Franklin?; Scholastic, 1976)*

> *In 1735 there were in Boston 42 streets, 36 lanes, 22 alleys, 1,000 brick houses, 2,000 wooden houses, 12 churches, 4 schools, 418 horses (at last count), and so many dogs that a law was passed prohibiting people from having dogs that were more than 10 inches high.*
> *(And Then What Happened, Paul Revere?, Scholastic; 1973)*

APPLYING THIS KNOWLEDGE TO NONFICTION

"The beaver's kits (babies) are kind of lucky because the kits are born with full hair and with their eyes partly open." This was the way Kellen began his response to our study of beavers, and it really caught my attention. We had been studying the mountain men of Colorado and their impact on the beaver population. As I read through his response, it was evident that he knew a lot about beavers.

Each time students write a response to a topic they have been studying in the content areas, I remind them to begin their entry with great lead sentences as Jean Fritz does. We also brainstorm different phrases that they could use, and I try to use these expressions as I am talking. Some students may begin their responses with long compli-cated sentences as Jean Fritz uses, but many use phrases such as: *It amazed me, Compared to, It is hard to believe* and so on. I've noticed that students not only write better lead sentences after these lessons, they also discuss a topic with more flair and color.

Evaluation

TEACHER EVALUATION

As I read through students' responses in the content areas and read their fiction and nonfiction stories, I make comments in my anecdotal notes on the use of strong lead sentences. Observing lead sentences in different types of writing gives me evidence of growth in this area. If I notice that certain students still have difficulty with this writing skill, I group them together. I again read samples of good lead sentences to this small group, and we work together revising the lead sentences they have written.

STUDENT EVALUATION

When all the students are writing a particular type of literature, such as tall tales, they take turns reading their lead sentences. Their peers give positive comments as well as offer suggestions for ways to make the sentences even better.

My students always share their writing with each other before they share it with me. After these lessons on writing great lead sentences, students seem to make a special effort to examine how their work opens. Together, students work to improve the lead sentences.

CHAPTER 14

Writing Plurals

OBJECTIVE   Students will discover the different ways words are made plural.

C hris came to me during reading workshop waving his copy of *Cowboys of the West* by Russell Freedman (Scholastic, 1985) and saying he'd found a mistake. He was convinced that the author had misspelled the word buffalo. He read aloud this passage to prove his point:

As the demand for beef grew, the cattle-raising industry spread northward from Texas. New ranches began to spring up all across the northern plains, where only a few years before herds of buffalo had grazed. By the 1870s, most of the buffalo had been slaughtered. They were replaced by longhorn cattle brought up the trails from Texas. Soon, a vast tract of cattle country stretched from Colorado up through Wyoming, Montana, and the Dakotas.

Chris was certain that buffalo was singular and the word needed an *s* to make it plural. He was positive he had seen it spelled that way in another source he had been reading.

135

Together we got out the dictionary and looked up the word *buffalo*. The *Webster's Encyclopedic Unabridged Dictionary of the English Language* said:

buffalo, n, pl. –loes, –los, –lo

Chris discovered that he and Russell Freedman were both right, and I realized once again how powerful trade books are for teaching reading and writing skills.

How I Do It

To prepare for the lesson, I cut out several dozen 2-by-4-inch pieces of paper. I tell students that the objective for this activity is to locate plural nouns and classify them according to the way the plural is formed. I rattle off a list of nouns such as *airplane, fish, turkey, microscope,* and *planet.* I ask students what part of speech these words represent. If there is any confusion about nouns, I review nouns before going further into the lesson.

Then I launch a back-and-forth game. I say, "one picture," and I ask a student to complete "three _____." The student responds "three pictures." I go back and forth with other nouns. I say the singular and the students say the plural after I give them a numerical digit to put in front of it. I don't dwell very long on this activity as it is only to place the idea of plural nouns in their train of thought. I try to stimulate interest by challenging students with unusual plurals such as *handful (handfuls)* and *sister-in-law (sisters-in-law).*

I next send students searching through the books they are reading to locate plural nouns. As they find them they write each one on a strip of paper, using a marker and large script. After a few minutes, I open up the search to include unusual plural words they can think of—they don't have to be in books.

Next I divide the class into groups of three or four and have them pool their words. As a group, they are to arrange their words into categories based on plural endings. After students have had an opportunity to categorize their words, they share their discoveries. As each group shares, I write their discoveries on the blackboard or chart paper. Common categories are:

- add *s* to the word
- add *es* to the word
- the word stays the same

◆ change the *y* to *i* and add *es*

◆ change the *f* to *v* and add *es*

If possible, I reserve a large wall area in the room where the words can be displayed in their categories. We write headings for the categories, and the students place their word strips under the correct category. After all the words are taped to the wall, I read aloud *Merry-Go-Round* by Ruth Heller (Scholastic, 1990). Through her art, her word choices, and her rhymes, Ruth Heller provides students with a variety of nouns and their plurals. This book helps students identify more categories to add to their Wall of Plurals.

I leave the Wall of Plurals on display as long as possible, and encourage students to add to it as they find plurals, especially unusual ones.

One year I did not have enough wall space so I made plural trees by anchoring tree branches in coffee cans with sand. On each can students wrote the plural heading. The slips of papers with the plural words were hung on the trees like leaves. We had *s* trees, *es* trees, *ies* trees, and a variety of irregular trees.

Students searching for plural nouns to add to our Wall of Plurals.

As a wrap-up to the lesson, I have students write what they know about forming plurals in their learning logs. I ask them to include specific examples in their discussion and to include the rules for forming plurals. The learning logs help students focus on the lesson and what they have learned. Many students use this response as a reference when they are uncertain about how to make a word plural.

Follow-Up Activities

USING THE DICTIONARY

I developed this lesson to help students learn to use the dictionary to find out how to write a plural. First I ask students to look up a specific word such as *hippopotamus*. After everyone has found *hippopotamus,* we examine the first part of the definition, looking at the abbreviation for plural (pl) and then the plurals immediately after it. Some students need help to understand that only the last syllable is written in the plural form. In this case, -*muses* or -*mi*. To clarify this concept—and to give students the chance to hear how these plurals sound when spoken—I have some students use the plural of *hippopotamus* in sentences and other students write the plural on the chalkboard.

The next word I like to have them locate is *octopus*. The dictionary shows that there are two ways to form the plural. Again students notice that only the last syllable is shown written in the plural form, -*puses* or -*pi*. Ruth Heller used octopus as an example in her book, *Merry-Go-Round,* so I reread that section of the book. She mentions that this word is derived from Latin or Greek. We locate that information in our dictionaries.

As a closure to this lesson I encourage students to suggest other plural nouns we should locate in our dictionaries. I always hear, "But it doesn't tell me how to make the plural." I like to throw the question right back at the class. "Why do you think it doesn't tell you? They soon realize that the dictionary only shows irregular plurals.

SPELLING

When I am teaching plurals, I also incorporate plural words into the spelling list for the week.

Evaluation

TEACHER EVALUATION

Work samples are a wonderful source of information on how my students are using plurals in their written work. I systematically examine their writings for evidence of growth in using plurals correctly. If I see a need for more instruction, I group students with like needs together for short reteaching lessons.

STUDENT EVALUATIONS

My students are required to confer with each other before presenting a paper to me for revising and editing. During their conference the students notice the plural words and see if the plural form is spelled correctly. Together they apply the rules as well as look up words in the dictionary.

SPELLING TESTS

When plurals of words are in the list of spelling words, I observe if the student correctly spells the word. I have noticed that many students are able to memorize a spelling list for a test and still not use the correct spelling in their daily writing. Therefore, I prefer to base my evaluation on the strategies the students use to form plurals in their daily written work.

MASTERY CHECKLIST

When there is evidence that a student has mastered the skill of correctly writing the plural forms of words, it can be checked off on her or his Writing Mastery Checklist. Anecdotal notes can be used to determine when a student qualifies for mastery.

Skill _____ **Mastery Date** _____

Forms plurals correctly

   regular plurals _____

   irregular plurals _____

   student examples _____

CHAPTER 15

Possessive Nouns

OBJECTIVE   Students will understand the meaning of possessive nouns and know how to correctly use the apostrophe to show possession.

I had always been a believer in the theory of teach when the need arises—and the need certainly did arise with my students when it came to using apostrophes in their writing. One of my students wrote:

> The Greeks' land was very rugged with mountains'. A lot of their land was near the sea. Since a lot of the land was near the sea, Greek's decided to take advantage of it. They got fish and crabs' from the sea.

How I Do It

When I began planning this lesson, I thought of Ruth Heller's books on the different parts of speech. *Merry-Go-Round, A Book About Nouns* (Grosset & Dunlap, 1990) was perfectly suited for this lesson. Ideally, I round up enough copies so that groups of two or three students can share it during the lesson. If that's not possible, I gather students close to me so everyone can see.

After students and I have enjoyed the book, I copy these two pages that refer to possessive nouns onto a chart:

Add apostrophe S's when NOUNS are POSSESSIVE, except when they're PLURALS ending in S's...*the tiger's stripes, the lion's mane, the camels' obvious disdain.*

I invite students to illustrate the chart with a lion, a tiger, and several camels. This illustrated, short passage becomes a colorful reference for us as we continue our study on when and how to use apostrophes to denote possession.

During my years of teaching, I have seen many students confuse the apostrophe in contractions with the apostrophe in possessives. To help them understand the difference, I look for pages in their trade books that illustrate the use of contractions and possessive nouns. I then make transparencies of these pages.

One of my students had done a book talk on *Whipping Boy* by Sid Fleischman, so I decided to work with a passage from that book. After a quick summary of the story for those who hadn't read it, we were all working with familiar material. It is important that skills be taught in context with familiar material.

After I place the transparency on the overhead projector, I ask a student to underline all the words in the passage that contain an apostrophe.

Cutwater rummaged around in a black oak chest of stolen goods. Handkerchiefs flew out like soiled white does, worn shoes, <u>ladies'</u> combs, a cowbell—a junk heap. <u>They've</u> had lean pickings, this raggedy pair of highwaymen, Jemmy thought. And maybe not as smart and clever as the song sellers made out.

"<u>Here's</u> a scrap of paper, Billy," said Cutwater, finding it in the pocket of a stolen coat. "But how are we going to do the scribblement? We <u>can't</u> write."

"<u>I've</u> seen it done. Sharpen us a <u>hawk's</u> feather, Cutwater."

Then we begin analyzing the words. The conversation between students and myself often goes like this.

MRS. L: The first word we have underlined is *ladies'*. How is the apostrophe used in that word?

JANINE: It tells us that the combs belonged to the ladies.

MRS. L: From those two words, Janine, can you tell us if there are one or more combs and/or one or more ladies?

JANINE: *Ladies* and *combs* are both plural so there are at least two combs and ladies.

MRS. L: I'm going to write *ladies' combs* on this chart before we look at the next word.

TONY: The next underlined word is a contraction.

MRS. L: What two words does it stand for?

TONY: *They have.*

MRS. L: I want to write *they've* on the chart. Is it in the same category as *ladies' combs*?

Through this type of interaction we soon have the words with apostrophes listed in two categories on a chart.

Examples of How Apostrophes Are Used

POSSESSION	CONTRACTIONS
ladies' combs	they've = they have
hawk's feather	here's = here is
	can't = cannot
	I've = I have

To examine this concept even further, I take an excerpt from *The Door in the Wall* by Marguerite de Angeli (Dell, 1949), a book we use when studying the Middle Ages. I place a transparency of the page on the overhead projector and continue the process of locating and charting all the words with apostrophes. This page is good because St. Mark's is an example of when the noun (church) is understood.

Brother Luke set Robin on the jennet, the robe and blankets around him making him comfortable. Brother Luke put a strap around <u>Robin's</u> waist, then ran under the <u>jennet's</u> belly to keep him from falling. He tied the bundle on at the back, and they set forth. Out through the door in the wall of the courtyard they went, into the street, Robin leaning against Brother Luke, and the jennet picking her way sedately over the cobbles.

There were not many people abroad, for it was the end of the day. Curfew was ringing as they returned up Creed Land to Ludgate Hill, and only because the guard knew <u>Brother Luke's</u> habit were they allowed to pass through the city gate. By then they were more than halfway to the hospice, but it was nearly dark when they reached <u>St. Mark's</u> and were admitted by the porter at the postern gate.

Again, students underline all the words that have an apostrophe. We then continue our dialogue and students discuss the words with apostrophes and add them to the chart in the correct category.

Examples of How Apostrophes Are Used

POSSESSION	CONTRACTIONS
ladies' combs	they've = they have
hawk's feather	here's = here is
jennet's belly	can't = cannot
Robin's waist	I've = I have
Brother Luke's habit	
St. Mark's (church)	

As a wrap-up to this lesson I have students look through the books they are reading independently to locate contractions that we don't have on the chart, as well as other examples of possessive nouns. As they locate words, they are encouraged to record them.

Poetry is another form of literature that I use to illustrate possessive words. One of my favorite poems for this lesson is "The Microscope" by Maxine Kumin. (I use this poem in science, too, so it is a good example of how to use literature across the curriculum.) After we have read and enjoyed the poem we look at all the words that show possession and those that are contractions. In the second verse we change the lines to read: *sheep's hair*, *lice's legs*, *people's skin*, and so on.

The Microscope

Anton Leeuwenhoek was Dutch.
He sold pincushions, cloth and such.
The waiting townsfolk fumed and fussed
As Anton's dry goods gathered dust.

He worked instead of tending store,
At grinding special lenses for
A microscope. Some of the things
He looked at were: mosquitoes' wings,
the hairs of sheep, the legs of lice,
the skin of people, dogs and mice:
ox eyes, spiders' spinning gear,
fishes' scales, a little smear
of his own blood, and best of all
the unknown, busy, very small
bugs that swim and bump and hop
inside a simple water drop.

Impossible! Most Dutchmen said..
This Anton's crazy in the head.
We ought to ship him off to Spain.
He says he's seen a housefly's brain.
He says the water that we drink
is full of bugs. He's mad, we think!

They called him dumkopf, which means dope.
That's how we got the microscope.

Maxine Kumin

When students understand that apostrophes are used in both contractions and possessives, I concentrate on the study of possessives and how singular and plural nouns are made possessive. The more students see possessives and are aware of how they are used, the more confident they become in using them in their writing. To give students immediate practice in using possessives correctly in their writing, I ask

145

them to use at least one possessive in a piece of writing on which they are working.

At the end of writing workshop I ask for volunteers to read sentences they wrote that contain possessives. After reviewing their pieces, I note who needs reteaching and form small groups for that purpose.

USE PROPS TO HELP VISUALIZE POSSESSION

Dramatization is a good learning tool for just about all children. I like to introduce this activity by putting on a crazy hat, the crazier the better. I usually wear my fishing hat complete with fishing lures on it. After I tell students that this is my hat, I ask them whose hat it is. The first answer is usually "your hat." I respond, "What is my name?" "Mrs. Laase's hat" is the answer I hear. I have a student write it on the board. Then I suggest that they might not know me. How could they describe the hat then?

> the teacher's hat
>
> the lady's hat
>
> the woman's hat

Each time they make a suggestion I have it written on the board, noting where the apostrophe is located.

Suddenly I pull out two more hats and add them to my first hat. Following the same procedure we write:

> Mrs. Laase's hats
>
> the teacher's hats
>
> the woman's hats

We note that the way the noun is written to show possession ('s) did not change even when we had more than one hat.

I then put the hats on three girls and ask them to come to the front of the room. I ask the students to tell us who owns the hats now. I write the words on the chalkboard as they say:

the girls' hats
the ladies' hats
the women's hats
the students' hats
the children's hats

We examine how the apostrophe comes after the *s* in a plural noun that ends in *s* and before the *s* in an irregular plural noun, such as *children's*. We have had a lot of fun, and the students have a visual picture of how possessives are written.

I then divide the class into groups and challenge each to look around the room and locate props such as books, pencils, coats, bookbags, lunches, and so on, that they can use to illustrate a possessive noun like I used my hats. A group at a time comes forward and uses their props to dramatize a possessive noun. To vary the activity, the groups can write the words on pieces of paper instead of on the chalkboard. Points can be given to groups who get them correct.

Follow-Up Activities

RESPONDING IN THE READING JOURNAL

After this activity I have students write in their Reading Journals. They are to discuss what they know and what they learned about possessives. I encourage them to look through the books they are reading and the material they are writing for samples to support their statements.

DEVELOP RULES FOR USING AN APOSTROPHE TO SHOW POSSESSION

To reinforce this concept, small groups of two or three students develop rules to follow when using an apostrophe to denote possession. After each group shares its rules, we list the rules on a chart for reference.

BULLETIN BOARD

I allocate a space on the classroom wall as our possessive wall. I divide the space into two sections—singular and plural. As the students find possessive words in the books they are reading, they record them on index cards and tape them to the wall under the correct section.

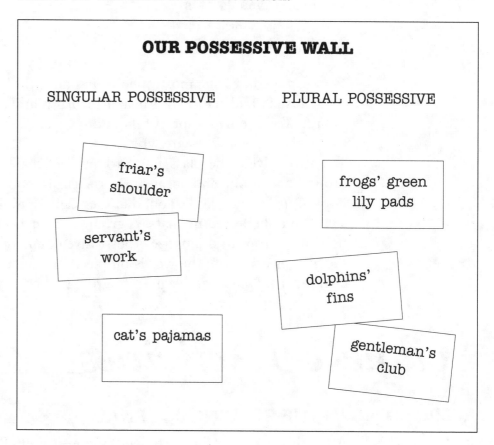

Evaluation

TEACHER EVALUATION

As I observe students' work, I note how they are using possessives. As I confer with each student, I praise a job well done. If apostrophes are missing, I may suggest that the student look at the word and see what has been left out. Frequently that's all that is needed. If the concept of writing a possessive noun correctly is still unclear, individual or small-group reteaching is necessary.

STUDENT EVALUATION

My students confer with each other before they bring a piece of writing to me. In addition to any other editing that is needed, they check that possessives are written correctly. When students confer with each other, they can help each other to apply the rules for using apostrophes correctly.

ANECDOTAL NOTES

I use my anecdotal notes to keep track of who understands this skill and who needs to join reteaching or review groups. I find that my anecdotal notes help me keep track of my students' progress. Students who need additional help are easily identified.

MASTERY CHECKLIST

When there is evidence that a student has mastered the skill of using an apostrophe correctly, it can be checked off on his or her Writing Mastery Checklist.

Skill _____ **Mastery Date** _____

Uses apostrophes in possessive nouns correctly.

    singular _____

    plural _____

    irregular _____

CHAPTER 16

Developing Vocabulary Using a Semantic Map

OBJECTIVE   Students will broaden their vocabulary and understanding of word relationships through the construction of a semantic map.

Semantic mapping is one of my favorite methods for teaching vocabulary. In this mini-lesson students become actively involved in learning new words, and they also strengthen their understanding of the concept to which the vocabulary is related. This method is not a new approach to vocabulary instruction, but it is one that is highly effective and motivational for the students.

During a semantic mapping lesson, students build a web of words related to a concept that we are studying. By identifying the unique relationships of certain words to the concept and by grouping related words, students accomplish several learning objectives: They broaden their vocabulary, they discover the interrelatedness of ideas, they sharpen their critical thinking skills, and they gain further understanding of the content.

The theory that supports and explains semantic mapping as an effective method of vocabulary and concept instruction can be found in *Concepts in the Social Studies*, edited by Barry Beyer and Anthony Penna (National Council for the Social Studies, 1971); *Models of Teaching* by Bruce Joyce and Marsha Weil (Prentice-Hall, Inc., 1980); and *Teaching Vocabulary to Improve Reading Comprehension* by William Nagy (NCTE, 1988).

How I Do It

Prior to the lesson, I prepare enough paper of approximately 52 by 24 inches for each group of three or four students to have one sheet. I also have colored markers and a large sheet of paper, about 72 by 36 inches on hand.

BRAINSTORMING

After students have had several lessons in a unit of study and have done some reading about the topic or concept, I introduce this mini-lesson by writing the major word or term related to our unit of study on a large sheet of paper. For instance, when we were studying the Constitution, I wrote *Constitution* on chart paper, and wrote *Nutrition* when we were studying that unit in health. Likewise, I used *Revolution* when we were studying the American Revolution and *Exploration* when we were studying the early explorers. The word can also be the title of the theme the class is studying.

Next, I ask students to brainstorm all the words they can think of which are related to the term. As they brainstorm, I list the words under the title. When we have a healthy list of words, it's time to categorize them.

CATEGORIZING

The students and I discuss the meaning of category—a group of things having several attributes in common. As an example of categorization, we discuss how we can categorize or group the students in the classroom and what the attributes of each group might be. Next, I ask students to study the words they have brainstormed and, based on their knowledge of the topic, suggest a category in which some of the words will fit because of their similar attributes. I write the category on the chalkboard. As they suggest words from the brainstormed list that fit in that category, I lead them in a discussion of the meanings of

the words and why they fit in this category.

In the next part of the lesson I have students work in small cooperative groups of about three or four. I explain that they are to discuss ways they can categorize the words which remain on the list. They are to write the category headings they select on their sheet of paper. Groups are also expected to discuss the meanings of the words and the attributes of the categories, and then write the words under the appropriate categories.

During discussion, students may find that some words do not fit in any category. Such a discovery is perfectly appropriate because part of the process of concept acquisition is the definition of concept boundaries. As students explore the idea that some words are not essential to understanding a particular topic, they refine their definition of the concept. Likewise, some categories may seem similar or closely related, and students have to think hard about whether to combine categories or to keep them separate. This critical thinking sharpens their appreciation of the concept and the words related to it.

EXPLORERS

Vasco da Gama
Vikings
Magellan
Marco Polo
Christopher Columbus
Prince Henry

PLACES

Africa
Portugal
Spain
North America
Newfoundland
India

EXPLORATION

TOOLS

sundial
compass
stars
charts
ships
logs

GOODS

glass beads
food
clothes
silk
spices
tea

I have the groups share their lists and explain the attributes of the various categories. To help them refine their understanding of the concept, I lead the class in a discussion of the various categories. I have the class come to a consensus on the most appropriate rules to use in determining which words belong in which category. We then decide which categories are the most important to studying the concept. Thus, students are prompted to think collaboratively and critically about a topic.

MAPPING

I then use the large sheet of 72-by-36-inch paper to complete a class semantic map. We place the categories we have developed on the paper and draw connecting lines between the categories that seem related to each other. I post the map, and students add additional words to the appropriate categories until the conclusion of the unit. This big poster makes the children's abstract thinking concrete. The semantic map also serves as a reference for the students as they engage in writing activities associated with the unit of study.

Later in the year, we may return to our original semantic map and apply it to a new unit. As students are prompted to relate the concept to a new setting or to additional information, they reinforce the validity of some of their categories and they refine or expand others. Students find that concepts are not static definitions, but ever-expanding sets of ideas that we use to organize our knowledge.

Summary

The semantic map is an excellent source of information for my students as they discuss and write about ideas related to the unit. I encourage them to refer to the maps for assistance with vocabulary and spelling. As I read their writings, I note the usage and understanding of the vocabulary, as well as the comprehension of the concepts. I provide additional instruction as needed to clarify misconceptions.

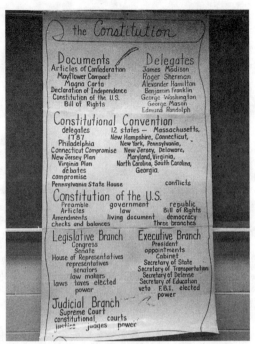

United States Constitution semantic map

All of my students benefit from semantic maps, but the maps are a particularly powerful language-acquisition tool for students whose primary language is not English and for students who infrequently use standard English. Often, a limited vocabulary frustrates these students when a new unit is taught. By working with other students to fit words in a semantic map, these students are provided with a classroom vocabulary reference that they have helped to create. I find that their own word repertoire expands as they deal with the concept. Furthermore, they conclude the unit with a concept they have truly acquired and a method for refining it that serves them throughout their learning years.

Evaluation

TEACHER EVALUATION

As my students categorize the words on their semantic maps, I observe them working and give assistance as needed. If there is a misunderstanding about the meaning of a word, I help them with the definition or with any misunderstanding related to the concept. I write anecdotal notes concerning their participation as group members. I observe the groups' explanations of how they categorized the words and how they discuss the attributes of the categories. I also use their writings to evaluate their understanding of the vocabulary and their comprehension of the concepts.

STUDENT EVALUATION

After the groups finish their semantic maps, they share them with the class and explain how they categorized the words and the attributes of each category. As an added challenge, I ask them to write a definition of the concept using some of the categories they have created. I also have them evaluate how they worked together as a group.

NOTES

NOTES

NOTES

NOTES

ABOUT THE AUTHORS

Joan Clemmons

Joan Clemmons, who lives in Montclair, Virginia, is a fifth-grade teacher and a past Teacher of the Year at Rolling Valley Elementary School in Fairfax County, Virginia. She is the co-author of *Portfolios in the Classroom: A Teacher's Sourcebook* and a member of the development team for the newly published language arts curriculum guide for Fairfax County Public Schools, the nation's tenth largest school district.

As a language arts consultant, lecturer, and workshop leader, she has made presentations regarding integrated language arts and portfolio assessment to a variety of audiences across the country, including the International Reading Association and the National Council of Teachers of English. Mrs. Clemmons is featured in Making Meaning, a video series from the Association for Supervision and Curriculum Development on organizing and assessing integrated language arts. She has been a contributor to *Portfolio News* and a resource to many teachers who have observed in her reading and writing classroom. In addition to teaching fifth grade, she has taught grades three through twelve.

Lois Laase

Lois Laase lives in Grand Junction, Colorado, where she is a teacher at Wingate Elementary School. She also teaches courses for Adams State College, in Alamosa, Colorado. She has had classroom experience is several other states, as well as International Schools in Norway, Italy, and Brazil. While living in Australia and Brazil she was the Community Liaison Officer at the American Embassy.

Mrs. Laase has published whole language thematic units, a literature-based math series, and is co-author of *Portfolios in the Classroom: A Teacher's Sourcebook*. She has also been a contributor to *Portfolio News*. She is a consultant in the area of language arts and has shared her expertise on integrated language arts and portfolio assessment at local, state, and national conferences, including the National Council of Teachers of English, the National Council of Teachers of Mathematics, and the International Reading Association. She is listed in *Two Thousand Notable American Women* and *Who's Who in American Education*, 1992–93 and 1993–94.